Date Due

SUICIDE

SUICIDE

Margaret O. Hyde and
Elizabeth Held Forsyth, M.D.

Third Edition

Franklin Watts 1991
New York London Toronto Sydney

Grateful acknowledgment is made for permission to
reprint from "Hopelessness: An Indicator of Suicidal Risk,"
by M. Kovacs, A. T. Beck, and M. A. Weissman, published
in *Suicide,* vol. 5, no. 2, copyright © 1975. The authors
would also like to thank the American Association of
Suicidology for providing the list of suicide-prevention centers.

This book has been revised and updated from
the previous edition, originally published
under the title *Suicide: The Hidden Epidemic* (Revised Edition)
by Margaret O. Hyde and Elizabeth Held
Forsyth, M.D., published in 1986.

Graphs by Vantage Art, Inc.

Library of Congress Cataloging-in-Publication Data
Hyde, Margaret O. (Margaret Oldroyd), 1917–   .
Suicide / Margaret O. Hyde and Elizabeth Held Forsyth. — Rev. ed.
p.   cm.
Includes bibliographical references and index.
Summary: Examines the various types of suicide and reasons why many
young people have taken their lives, suggesting ways to prevent this
growing epidemic.
ISBN 0-531-11003-6
1. Suicidal behavior—Juvenile literature. 2. Youth—Suicidal behavior—
Prevention—Juvenile literature. [1. Suicide.]
I. Forsyth, Elizabeth Held. II. Title.
RC569.H898   1991
616.85′445—dc20   90-46872   CIP   AC

Contents

SUICIDE

1
Teen Suicide: A Continuing Mystery

Someone you know may be trying to take his or her life at this very moment.

Sometimes, it seems that suicide is happening everywhere, but it is actually relatively rare. This is true, even though about 1,500 teens in the United States attempt suicide every day, and about sixteen of them succeed within each twenty-four hour period.[1] This means that one young person commits suicide about every hour and a half. Considering the number of young people in the United States, this is not very many. However, if you knew that person, or even read about that person, suicide seems important. And it really is, since there is a good chance that the suicide could have been prevented.

Suicide is not only a personal tragedy. It profoundly affects a wide circle of family, friends, and acquaintances. The entire community may feel that they somehow failed that person.

As many as 70 percent of a large number of people who were questioned in connection with a survey of suicide behavior have indicated that suicide has

9

touched their lives because of the actions of friends and relatives. No wonder so many people want to do something about these tragic and unnecessary deaths.

The following cases of suicide might be reported in the newspapers of almost any large city during almost any month of the year:

A young celebrity enjoys success but suffers from personal pressures and problems. After spending an evening chatting with friends, he shoots himself in the head with a pistol.

A young man throws himself in front of a train with the obvious intent of committing suicide. A year later, on the anniversary of the young man's death, a girl who loved him follows the same pattern of action.

A girl's father dies when she is ten years old. For the next few years she is moody. Sometimes she is sad about her father's death. Sometimes she is angry at him because he left her. One night she writes a note saying that she is going to be with her father and she takes an overdose of sleeping pills.

Why do these people take their own lives? Could these deaths have been prevented? Many people have explanations as to what happened and why it happened. The experts are more cautious. They know that suicide is the result of many different and complex factors and that each case is unique.

For some people, the subject of suicide contains a certain fascination. For others, the subject is just too horrible to think about. Fortunately, a great many people, perhaps like you, are interested in learning about what can be done to help the desperate, lonely, and often confused people who attempt to take their own lives.

There are more questions about suicide than answers. Do people have the right to commit suicide? Do those who feel that they no longer want to live really want to die? How can they be helped? What causes them to choose suicide? Will reading about suicide cause people to take their own lives? You can find the answers to some of these questions as you read later chapters in this book. You can be sure right now that reading about suicide is not one of the causes. In fact, just the opposite may be true. For those people who exhibit self-destructive behavior to a serious degree, becoming aware of their intentions tends to decrease the chances of suicide. Refusing to discuss suicide with a person who is considering it frustrates attempts at communication. Open and honest discussion can be the first step in suicide prevention.

Experts believe that a key factor in preventing suicide is to help people tell the difference between the well-established facts and the fallacies. Suicide is a subject steeped in erroneous folklore, superstitions, and myths. Many of the false ideas are dangerous because they obstruct the recognition of danger signals.

Suicide need not be America's unspoken tragedy. Knowledge about suicide may save thousands of lives, perhaps even someone you know. You may be the vital link that assures help or professional assistance for a person who does not really want to die but who can no longer tolerate feelings of hopelessness, helplessness, and emotional isolation. The choice of life is the alternative to suicide. You may help point the way to it.

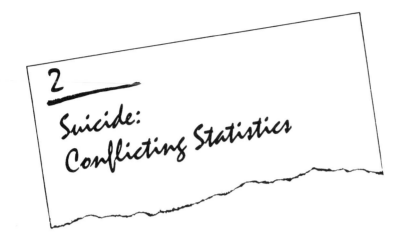

2
Suicide: Conflicting Statistics

Has there been an increase in the amount of adolescent suicide? Most experts believe so, and that the rate is alarming. As the graph on page 13 shows, the 1989 *Report of the Secretary's Task Force on Youth Suicide* states that suicide among young persons ages fifteen to twenty-four has more than doubled between 1950 and 1980.[2] Some experts believe it has even tripled. Certainly, the suicide rate among the young has increased to the point where it has created both controversy and concern.

Suicide was considered the second cause of death for the fifteen-to-twenty-four age group, before the tremendous increase in drug violence boosted homicide rates to record heights in 1990. Only accidents claimed more lives than homicides and suicides.[3] In spite of the extensive study conducted by the Task Force on Youth Suicide, much remains to be learned about suicide, including how common it is and why the rate increases and decreases.

Young people still have one of the lowest suicide rates of any age group, but the self-inflicted death of

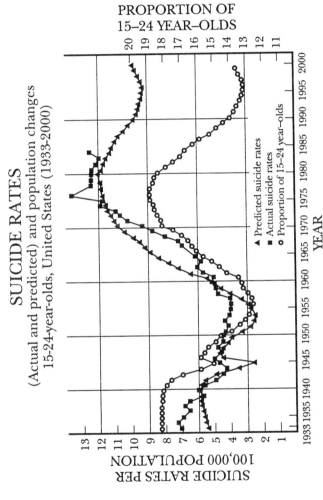

SUICIDE RATES
(Actual and predicted) and population changes
15–24-year-olds, United States (1933-2000)

**PROPORTION OF
15–24 YEAR–OLDS**

▲ Predicted suicide rates
■ Actual suicide rates
○ Proportion of 15–24 year–olds

YEAR

SUICIDE RATES PER
100,000 POPULATION

Source: Report of the Secretary's Task Force on Youth Suicide, U.S. Department of
Health and Human Services, 1989.

young people varies both in rate and time. Perhaps suicide prevention centers played a major role in the decrease in the suicide rate between 1979 and 1985. A decrease in the number of adolescents in proportion to the rest of the population during these years also may have played a part. But the number of adolescents is expected to rise during the 1990s, and the rate of suicide among the young is also expected to increase. While experts disagree about which and how many young people take their own lives, they do agree that suicide occurs frequently enough to be considered an important public health problem in the United States today.

UNDERREPORTING

Suicides are generally underreported. The actual number may be twice what it appears to be. In many cases, it is difficult to determine whether or not a person really meant to take his or her own life. Consider the case of Mary. She was attractive, sensitive, a good student, popular with her friends, and full of promise. One morning she mysteriously drove her car off the cliffs of the Pacific Palisades in Los Angeles. Did she do this on purpose or was it a freak accident? The autopsy showed no evidence of a physical problem, there was no suicide note, there seemed to be no explanation.

Experts believe that many deaths, including drug overdoses, poisonings, homicides, falls, and single car crashes, may actually be misclassified suicides. Even violent behavior can be potentially self-destructive. Sometimes suicides are reported as accidents, or even as homicides, to protect families and friends from the pain and stigma that still surround suicide.

14

CHILDREN WHO COMMIT SUICIDE

Determining if suicide is a cause of death is especially difficult in the case of young children. For many years, experts believed that children could not take their own lives. They said that children by nature are too small, too weak, and lack sufficient motor coordination and access to the resources needed to take their own lives. Today, such beliefs are slowly being disproved.

Most children below the age of ten do not realize that death is final, and completed suicide among young children is rare. Yet there *have* been cases of suicide among young children. Very young children are more likely to run in front of cars or trucks, or to jump from high buildings or cliffs. Children above the age of nine are more likely to take lethal doses of medicine, toxic materials used for cleaning, bug killers, or rubbing alcohol, or even large amounts of some harmless material, such as turtle food, that can be lethal when ingested in large quantities.

Even though parents, other relatives, and neighbors find a childhood suicide difficult to comprehend, experts suggest that suicidal fantasies, acts, and threats must be taken seriously in children as young as three years of age.[4] Suicide is considered the fifth leading cause of death in children between the ages of five and fourteen, but this may be a vast understatement since most suicides in children are probably not identified as such.[5]

THE WISH TO DIE

Suicide among the young is more common among males than females by a ratio of 5 to 1. A 1988 National Adolescent Student Health Survey, funded primarily by the U.S. Public Health Service, reported that one in seven students in the study had attempted suicide.[6] Other studies suggest that the ratio of attempts of males to females under nineteen (approximately) 4 to 1, but this rate decreases for the total population.[7] Between one and ten of all attempters go on to commit suicide, but no one knows how many people who attempt suicide really *want* to complete it.

Excluding cases wherein a deranged individual acts against him- or herself or faces a terminal illness, the decision to commit suicide is almost always a combination of a wish to live and a wish to die. This is called "ambivalence." A person who is suicidal usually leaves a message or a trail of signs that hint of his or her intentions. Some of the signs may be subtle, but they may be recognized as a cry for help by someone who knows how to read them. However, even a trained professional may miss the warning signs until after the fact. An adolescent suicide may easily be viewed as an accident, an undetermined death, or even a homicide. Certainly, statistics on suicide are conflicting.

PROBLEMS OF INTERPRETATION

One of the difficulties with suicide statistics is the obvious problem of not being able to communicate with the person who has taken his or her life. Even when notes are left, the content may not offer much information about the seriousness of the attempt, leaving some question as to whether or not the death was accidental. If the cause of death is not clear, many people choose to claim death by natural causes in order to avoid stigma for the family of the victim. The following cases illustrate how interpretations vary.

Situation ■ A man, age thirty-five, was warned that continued drinking would surely kill him since his liver and digestive system were already damaged. He con-

16

tinued to drink heavily, and died within a year of the warnings. The cause of death was listed as natural.

Situation ▪ A woman, age twenty-five, was depressed over her career situation. She threatened suicide several times. While driving her car, she crashed into a tree. No skid marks were observed, indicating she had not tried to brake the car. The cause of death was listed as accidental.

Situation ▪ A man, age twenty, formerly had been a patient in a mental hospital. He had been diagnosed as schizophrenic but had shown definite improvement in recent weeks. He jumped or fell from a window on the tenth floor of his apartment building. The cause of death was never determined.

Situation ▪ A woman, age nineteen, wanted to manipulate her father into buying a car. She left a note saying that she had taken an overdose of barbiturates and was sorry that her father could not understand her inability to live without a car. She arranged to be in a hallway where her father always entered the house on returning from work at 5 P.M. The woman took the pills just before 5 P.M. but her father was delayed that day and no one came home until 8 P.M. The cause of death was listed as suicide.

HIDDEN SUICIDES

In addition to the confusing picture that would result from any statistics compiled from the above situations, there are numerous kinds of hidden suicides. People who take great risks, who overeat, drink too much, experiment with drugs, smoke too much, and indulge in other forms of self-destructive behavior might be counted as unconscious or slow suicides. There are

17

people who precipitate their murder as a form of suicide.

STATISTICS AND PEOPLE

Large numbers of charts exist that reveal the statistics on those who committed suicide in different years and different places. These charts contain such classifications as locality (urban or rural); sex; race; time of the year, month, and day; and so forth. Some of these charts help suicidologists to observe trends and are useful in research. But a look at the problems of families and the individual people in them may be more meaningful than all the statistics in the world.

3
Patterns of Suicide

Often one does not know the full circumstances behind a suicide, since each individual is unique. Feelings of inferiority and worthlessness, depression, hopelessness, or wanting to cause guilt feelings in others are just some of the emotions that may make people flirt with death. But even though each case is complex, there appear to be common situations that act as triggers for the event. Examining patterns of suicide may help us to recognize danger signals and provide some insight into its causes. Have you read about any suicides that seem to fit into the following patterns?

ATTEMPTS TO MANIPULATE OTHERS

In many cases of suicide, the person tries to manipulate very important or significant people in his or her environment by producing guilt feelings in them. Consider the case of a young boy who desperately wants a car of his own. He has tried all kinds of pleas, threats, and other behavior in efforts to get what he wants, but his parents do not buy the car for him. Since he is being treated by a doctor for his long-term depression, medication is in his bureau drawer. After consulting the doctor about what would or would not be a lethal dose of his medicine under the guise of a friend's wanting to know, the boy takes enough pills to scare his parents. He is gambling with death, but he takes the risk. He believes that his parents will be so sorry when the nearly empty pill bottle is discovered that they will no longer deny him a car. They may think he will really try suicide again if they do not respond to his wish. If his manipulations or attempts at blackmail do not bring the desired results, the above episode may be repeated in a variety of ways. At some point, the boy may actually lose the gamble with death. Or he may reach a therapist who can help him sort out the disturbed feelings that cause him to make unrealistic demands.

While suicide in children is not common, some boys and girls over the age of five do attempt to manipulate parents, or others, in this way. Adults, too, may retain childish behavior and use attempted suicide as a form of manipulation either consciously or unconsciously. For them, too, plans may be upset and an accidental suicide may occur.

MAGICAL THINKING AND ATTEMPTS TO PUNISH

Some magical thinking can be present in the attempt to manipulate others. Another pattern of suicide that involves magical thinking occurs when a person considers suicide as a way to be completely powerful and in complete control. After all, if one cannot feel powerful in any other way, one *can* be master of the way in which one dies. Suicide can be viewed as an omnipotent act. This may seem to be somewhat like burning

20

down a house to get rid of an odor, but for people who are confused, desperate, and/or feeling utterly inferior, here is a way to experience power and to punish those who keep him or her from power in life.

Many children do not realize the finality of death and think that they will be present at their own funerals to enjoy the weeping parents or others who have punished the child in a way that was felt to be unjust. "You'll be sorry when I'm gone" is a frequent taunt of children who are powerless to return punishment. Since they are frustrated, they attempt to take revenge by fantasies of committing suicide. They picture how sorry a parent would be to see them dead and relish the remorse and guilt feelings they have caused. While relatively few children act out such fantasies, some do without realizing that they cannot return to life in some magic way.

Adults who are unable to express hostility in some direct way are more prone to fantasize about, or even attempt, suicide than those who can openly express aggression. An ancient Asian custom, rarely practiced today, shows this type of suicide quite clearly. A person who had suffered a severe emotional affront, especially from someone of a higher social class who could not be approached directly, might commit suicide on the enemy's doorstep. Many adults of other cultures have taken their lives and carry out apparent wishes to avenge themselves by making another person feel guilty. Although this wish to die may be greater than the desire to live, it often appears to be related to a denial of the finality of death.

THE ANNIVERSARY SUICIDE

An example of the anniversary suicide was mentioned on page 10. The girl who threw herself in front of the train exactly one year after the man she loved had

21

committed suicide this way is just one of many instances in which people attempt to join others who have taken this course of action. A person may follow the pattern of another by choosing the same day, the same method, or both. About one-third of those who attempt suicide seem to be influenced by the suicide of someone close to them. Perhaps the first suicide lowers the second person's restraints against this kind of act.

ACCIDENTAL SUICIDE

Some accidental deaths are expressions of an unconscious death wish. A person may be hemmed in by frustration and desperate loneliness but feels prevented from committing suicide because it is against one's religious beliefs or considered cowardly. Such a person may seek risks in which death appears to be accidental. For example, a driver who smashes a car into a tree may have driven carelessly because of some unconscious desire to die. A racing car driver may continue to race after having had a number of crashes until one is fatal.

Alcoholics rank high in the statistics of suicide. Some experts believe that the alcohol releases uncontrollable rage or discharge of impulses which results in suicide that often appears to be accidental. Drunken drivers who kill themselves in single car accidents are often considered to have unconscious suicidal wishes.

DRUG ABUSE

Alcohol is a drug commonly associated with suicide in several ways. Although alcohol is really a depressant, many suicide attempters have said they drank alcohol to "screw up enough courage" to perform the act. In addition to impairing a person's judgment and exag-

22

gerating his or her mood swings, alcohol is a contributing factor to some suicides through its effect on vital organs. In several studies, 15 to 50 percent of completed suicides were alcoholics.[8]

In addition to alcohol, barbiturates and anti-anxiety drugs are other depressants associated with suicide. Cocaine, especially crack, amphetamines (speed), and related drugs are stimulants that, like other mind drugs, can impair judgment, increase impulsiveness and anxiety, and induce hallucinations. Drug depressed or stimulated people are more likely to consider suicide because many of them do not realize that their feelings are drug related. Many, like Tom, believe that their feelings are a reaction to the way things really are. Tom was smoking crack whenever he could get it. He experienced cycles of highs and lows, but during one of his depressed periods, he decided it was easier to smash his car into a pole than to search for more crack. Without his drug-induced depression, Tom was a person who enjoyed playing the piano and pursuing his career as a lawyer.

The suicide rate among substance abusers is probably double that of the general population. The number of teens who commit suicide while drunk or using drugs other than alcohol is almost ten times as great as it was twenty years ago, according to *Do It Now* Publications.[9] Certainly, there is a strong link between substance abuse and suicidal behavior.

ROMANTIC SUICIDE

Death by suicide can be made tragically beautiful in literature, in movies, and on television, but the fact is that suicide is a sad and messy event. This never occurs to people who think their own deaths may achieve some romantic meaning.

Although suicide has often served as the climax of

23

many works of drama and fiction, in the book *Youth Suicide Prevention: Lessons from Literature,* the authors show that literature repeatedly treats the act of suicide as unromantic, wasteful, and unnecessary.

Many young people gain satisfaction in fantasies about death. They see it as a means of uniting with a friend, parent, or sibling who has died. Others think romantically of suicide as a way to punish loved ones, but seem not to realize that they will not be around to witness the impact of their death on the people they are trying to hurt.

Lovers' pacts are familiar to most readers as romantic suicides, but in many cases they are actually murder-suicides. Reports from survivors of such pacts suggest that one, usually the man, subtly or not so subtly coerces the partner to prove her love by dying with him.

Perhaps the most extreme case of coercion was the mass suicide that took place in Jonestown, Guyana, South America, in 1978.

MASS SUICIDES

Although some mass suicides in time of war are considered heroic, the tragedy at Jonestown, or the Guyana massacre, will never be fully understood. James Warren Jones, known commonly as Jim Jones, was a college dropout who became an unordained minister. He moved from church to church before founding the People's Temple in Indianapolis, Indiana.

Jones attracted a wide following of poor and idealistic people, about a hundred of whom followed him to Ukiah, California, after he convinced them that a nuclear attack would destroy Indiana. From there he moved to San Francisco, where his following grew and

24

Jones became a politically influential figure in the Bay area.

Jones claimed at times that he was the incarnation of Jesus healing the sick, and at other times that he was a reincarnation of V. I. Lenin, the Russian Marxist, arguing for social justice. He attracted large numbers of alienated people, both black and white, who worked for his cause by collecting contributions and gave much of their own money to the treasury of the People's Temple. This included the Social Security checks of many who believed in his work of social programs, which by now included an infirmary, child care center, carpentry shop, printing press, and kitchens which fed large numbers of people each day.

Jim Jones appeared to be a truly religious leader and champion of the poor. However, he was tightening his stranglehold on the vulnerable members of the People's Temple.

In 1973, Jones sent a twenty-member search party to Guyana to find a site where they could establish an agricultural mission for ghetto youth and others who could benefit from rural life. After a fire in the San Francisco temple and some scandals about Jones and his followers, about a thousand people followed him to the "promised land." Many of the people who were drawn by his magnetism and by difficult situations in their personal lives looked forward to communal living in a new land. But their diets were poor, the work was hard, and their leader periodically withdrew his support from any who strayed from total allegiance. Jones implanted suicidal thoughts in their minds over a period of time.

About five months before they committed mass suicide, the people, including children, were given a small glass of red liquid to drink. They were told that it contained poison and that they would die within forty-five minutes. When they did not, Jones explained that

25

this was a loyalty test and the time was not far off when they would take their own lives in a similar way. On November 18, 1978, 911 people died from drinking liquid poisoned with cyanide. Among the dead were more than 200 children. Although some of these people were probably forced to die, a substantial number of people willingly followed orders to poison themselves.

Some of those who died may have believed that they would make others sorry for not treating them better in an adolescent fantasy of revenge. But many were emotionally and physically exhausted and were suffering from malnutrition. The myth of the promised land led only to suicide.

IMITATIVE AND CLUSTER SUICIDES

A number of studies indicate that suicide news coverage and media dramas depicting suicides trigger a temporary increase in the number of young people who take their own lives. Imitative acts may occur throughout the country, or they may occur as cluster suicides in groups within a community. The vulnerable period usually lasts for about a week after a television event or after the death of a popular student, making this a time for counselors and teachers to be more alert to warning signs.

Cluster suicides are not a new phenomenon. Scores of young Germans took their own lives after reading a romantic story of unrequited love, Goethe's *The Sorrows of Young Werther,* published in 1774. There have been many cases of "copycat" suicides through the years, but recent ones have been more publicized.

When one teenager died in a car accident, it drew attention to seven other young people who took their own lives within the year. This was in the affluent suburb of Plano, near Dallas, Texas. In Westchester

County, New York, where there were thirty teen suicides in a period of two years, five teenagers ended their lives within a twenty-day period. In Clear Lake, Texas, six teenagers committed suicide within a span of fourteen months. News reports about cluster suicides alarm communities far and wide. Some ask if suicide might, in some mysterious way, be contagious.

Studies that link suicide with the effect of television-viewing are still controversial. While romanticized and sensational media coverage may confer an air of celebrity on those who commit suicide, researchers find no evidence that adolescents not already at risk of suicide are more likely to commit imitative suicides. Large memorial gatherings at schools and repeated media coverage tend to make those at risk more vulnerable since this gives them the impression that suicide is an act through which they can gain considerable attention from family and friends, even though they have some awareness that they will not be present to receive it. Perhaps many of these young people are so troubled that they do not fully understand the finality of their acts.

In some cases, publicity about suicides and sensitively written movies may have a positive effect, making people more aware of their own need to seek help. Some who imitate the suicide of a close relative feel that they have been "programmed" to follow the same pattern of behavior, and these people may be fated to follow the same script unless therapy prevents it.

HOMICIDE-SUICIDE

The idea of aggression turned outward as a cause of murder, and aggression turned inward as a cause of suicide is repeated again and again by experts who have explored the subjects of suicide and death. Karl Menninger, in *Man Against Himself,* describes three types of motivation for all suicides. They are a wish to kill, a wish to be killed, and a wish to die.

Consider the case of a young man who had appeared troubled for a number of years. One winter day, neighbors found him bleeding from stab wounds. He told people that he had been "jumped," but many people believed that the wounds were self-inflicted. About a year and a half later, the twenty-year-old man killed six people as they jogged, walked, or rode motorcycles near a railroad track. The killer dragged each body into the bushes and then waited for the next person to come along. When apprehended by the police, the man committed suicide. Authorities were at a loss to explain the slayings, but those who knew the man at school and in his neighborhood described him as a person who had been troubled for a long time. Here, and in many other cases, aggression turned outward resulted in the murder of others and aggression turned inward resulted in suicide. Of course, this does not explain why this person suffered from such aggression or expressed it in the tragic way that he chose.

HEROIC SUICIDES

For some cultures, the act of taking one's life is considered heroic. In previous times, the Japanese military class instilled the idea of the possible need for self-destruction in their children while they were very young. A situation in which honor was involved meant self-destruction without personal choice for the Japanese nobility of olden times. Such suicide, the best-known form of which is hara-kiri, was considered compulsory.

During World War II, Japanese kamikaze pilots crashed their planes against enemy targets for the good of their country. Soldiers far and wide in many wars have died for their ideals in a form of heroic suicide. Idealistic young people have died for many causes, some taking violent action in the cause of nonviolence. For example, Buddhist monks who bathed in gasoline, ignited themselves, and calmly burned to death were performing an act of self-destruction in their effort to communicate their message of protest against violent action.

In India today, a Hindu widow is forbidden by law to throw herself on the funeral pyre of her husband, but at one time this custom was practiced among women of the upper castes. This practice, known as suttee, was instilled in women from childhood and those who did not commit such heroic suicides lived in shame.

4
Why Suicide? Conflicting Theories

Whenever a person commits suicide, people ask why. The patterns of suicide show some of the circumstances that lead to the final act. None fully answers the question, Why suicide? This question has been asked long before people made an attempt to define what constitutes suicide. And it will continue to be asked far into the future.

DEFINITIONS OF SUICIDE

Even the word *suicide* is difficult to define. A common definition is "the act of intentionally destroying oneself." But there are instances in which a suicide occurs but another individual acts as the vehicle. The soldier who throws himself on a grenade to spare others does not fit the usual definition of intentional suicide. Many investigators define suicide as a violent, self-inflicted destructive action resulting in death. Medical-legal definitions of suicide include the concept of playing a major role in bringing about one's own death. A recent edition of the Oxford University Press Psychiatric

Dictionary defines suicide simply as "the act of killing oneself."

The word *suicide* is a relatively recent one. Although the exact date of its first use is not certain, it was probably introduced about the middle of the seventeenth century. Before that time, people referred to the act as self-murder, self-slaughter, self-destruction, and defined it with such expressions as "to cause violence to oneself," "to fail by one's own hand," "to procure one's own death," and so on.

Even today's professionals and researchers disagree among themselves about basic definitions of such terms as *suicide attempt, suicide gesture,* and *suicidal.* One coroner in the United States is reported to certify death as a suicide only if a note is found. Since the estimated percentage of suicides in which notes are left varies from 10 percent to 40 percent, the number of suicides reported by this coroner is vastly understated. One reason his figures are low may be his concern about the problems that a suicide creates for the family of the victim. Each relative and friend asks why, again and again. Many, like the coroner, want to deny that suicide occurred.

"Andy could not have deliberately jumped in front of that car," insists a mother whose son took his life. She can find no reason why.

"Kim could not have destroyed herself by reckless driving. She was so happy."

"He had so much to live for," is a remark that is commonly heard among those who continue to question why a person committed suicide. Why one and not another?

No one really knows why any person commits suicide and there is no single theory that satisfactorily explains the many possible causes of suicide. The suicidal act has been described as the end of a dark tunnel. Many people can describe an event, like the straw that broke the camel's back, that precipitated the attempt of suicide. But others do not know what triggered their attempts. Those who work with large numbers of people who have tried to take their lives admit they are mystified by many of the situations.

Why are some people suicidal while others are not—even when external stresses appear to be equal? Not every deeply depressed person commits suicide. Not everyone who feels helpless and hopeless is self-destructive. And not every self-destructive act can be interpreted as suicidal. Many people who indulge in some form of self-destructive behavior, such as heavy smoking, excessive use of alcohol, or overeating, are not motivated by the wish to die. They are careful with their health otherwise.

The search for a common denominator to suicide has been long and varied. Theories are numerous and many have overlapping features, but most scientific approaches are relatively modern. The earlier theorists were mostly concerned with the rightness or wrongness of the act rather than the causes.

Certainly, suicide evokes many inconsistent and contradictory feelings. The story of Kitty Jay is just one illustration, but it is a particularly interesting one because of tradition which is carried on to modern times. According to oral history, Kitty Jay was a foundling who lived in the middle of the eighteenth century. She was taken in by owners of one of the great houses on the moor in South Devon, England, and employed as a servant. Here she became romantically involved with one of the sons of the great house. When she became pregnant there was no possibility of marriage to the baby's father because of the class distinction. Usually a family helped such a girl financially, but in this particular case, no provision was made. Kitty Jay was to be turned out without the benefit of the care often provided in such situations. Her despair was so great that Kitty Jay hanged herself in a barn on the moor.

Even though there was no question of murder in the case of Kitty Jay, a coroner's jury was called to examine the case. They were to decide whether or not the girl was of sound mind at the time she hanged herself, for this would determine whether or not she could be buried in the churchyard. If she were of sound mind when she took her life, Kitty Jay could not be buried in consecrated ground. Since the jury ruled that this was the case, she was buried according to the custom of the time—at the crossroads where every beggar's foot might pass over her grave.

The attitude of the local people was one of sympathy for this person who had committed suicide. A headstone was placed at her grave and it was surrounded with stones as protection from the footsteps of those who walked at this crossroads on the moors. According to local tradition and folklore, each day someone has placed fresh wild flowers or greens on this grave for more than two centuries. No one suspects ghosts, but no one will tell who places the fresh flowers or greens there. Perhaps it is the descendants of the family whose illegitimate child died when Kitty Jay committed suicide. Certainly, Kitty Jay's suicide lived on in the memory of people for a long time. But neither the people nor the jury really gave the answer to the question, Why suicide?

From the time of Kitty Jay to today, many scientific studies and statistics have explored the question of why people take their own lives.

MORSELLI'S STUDIES

Henry Morselli, an Italian professor of psychological medicine, was an early investigator of the subject. He wrote a book called *Suicide: An Essay on Comparative*

Moral Statistics, which was originally published in Milan in 1879 and was reprinted in the United States in 1975 by Arno Press. He noted that there were many secret motives that eluded even the suicidal individuals themselves because they acted upon them unconsciously. Morselli explored many statistics and attempted to relate "cosmico-natural" influences (climate, geological formations, and so on), ethnological influences (races, nationalities), biological influences (sex, age), social conditions of the individual (civil status, profession, economic position, social status), and individual psychological influences. While many of Morselli's conclusions would be challenged today, his work was a beginning in the study of a subject that heretofore had been avoided.

DURKHEIM'S THEORY

Perhaps the most famous research into causes of suicide is Emile Durkheim's classical study. This was first published in French in 1897, and it continues to be important reading for any serious student of the subject. Durkheim, who lived from 1858 to 1917, grouped suicides into four basic patterns as follows: egoistic, altruistic, anomic, and fatalistic.

Egoistic suicide results when a person no longer finds a basis for existence in life. The person feels alienated from society, has too few ties with the community, and is suffering from loneliness and isolation. Most suicides in the United States fall into this category.

Altruistic suicide involves an opposite type of relationship. In some societies, where people are greatly bound and dedicated to a cause, suicide is considered honorable. These are "heroic suicides," such as those of the Japanese kamikaze pilots in World War II or the

34

fiery deaths of Buddhist priests in protest of the Vietnam War.

Anomic suicide is related to great change in a person's family relationship, career, health, or other important aspect of life. The term *anomie* literally means "deregulation." Sudden change for the better may also precipitate suicide. For example, a person who is promoted into a more demanding job may find it too stressful and use suicide as an escape. Or a person who wins a gold Olympic medal may feel there is nothing else to strive for.

Fatalistic suicide occurs among prisoners, slaves, or others in situations of excessive regulation.

These descriptions of Durkheim's categories are overly simplified, but they give one an idea of his approach to the study of suicide. According to Durkheim, the suicide rate is related to the strengths and weaknesses of society. The causes are external or environmentally determined. Suicide is considered a social disease and prevention dependent on social change. His various categories are described in some length in his book and are discussed and criticized in many other books. One of the most important contributions that Durkheim made in the area of suicide was to stimulate further research on the subject.

FREUD'S THEORIES

While Durkheim's theory points to the influence of the social situation on a person, Sigmund Freud (1856–1939) viewed suicidal urges as essentially a problem within the individual. Freud believed that life and death forces are in constant conflict in every person, even though these forces are unconscious. He explained suicide as the state wherein the death instinct wins over the life instinct.

Frustrations may cause the aggressive side of the

35

person's emotions to become directed inward. Murdering oneself is considered a way of killing the image of a person who is both loved and hated. In this sense, the suicidal individual identifies with the person he or she unconsciously wants to kill. Freud's studies on suicide were far more extensive than the ideas mentioned here. His theories were developed between the years 1881 and 1939.

Sylvia Plath, the poet and author of *The Bell Jar,* a novel that tells about a personal suicide attempt, lost her father when she was nine. Her poem "Daddy" is a vivid example of an intense struggle with ambivalent feelings about a dead parent. Freud argued that suicide was an outcome of the ego's struggle to cope with loss. Sylvia Plath's identification with the lost father involved mourning which turned inward because of ambivalent feelings of love and hate for her father. The split feelings can be exhausting, as in her case. She wrote in her poem of her desire to be "finally through" with her father and of the "vampire who said he was you." After flirting with death, through several earlier suicide attempts, this brilliant young woman died when a servant failed to enter her gas-filled kitchen at the time she was scheduled to arrive. Sylvia Plath left a note saying, "Please call Dr.____." His telephone number was included in the note, but it was too late when she was discovered. Her cry for help misfired because the gas drugged the man who lived on the floor beneath her and he could not be awakened to open the door for the servant. This risk-taking activity of Sylvia Plath is a vivid example of Freud's theory of ambivalence toward a lost parent, or love object, and of other theories about unfinished "grief work" in which there is an abnormal desire for reunion with a lost loved one. It is also a good example of the ambivalence of many would-be suicides.

ADLER'S THEORY

Alfred Adler lived from 1870 until 1937 and was considered an important figure in the world of psychology. He was one of the members of a group of psychoanalysts who followed Freud, but he broke away and developed his own concepts. He is most frequently associated with the concept of inferiority complex, and it is through this that he explains his theory of suicide. He describes the suicidal person as one who suffers from extreme feelings of inferiority, self-centered goals, and hidden aggression. The person, who is often the product of a pampered childhood, uses suicide as an attempt to manipulate people in an environment in which he or she is unable to relate satisfactorily to others. Adler argues that the suicidal person may see death as a way of proving worthlessness and showing others that he or she is not worth caring for. For some, suicide may offer increased self-esteem through mastery over life and death.

MENNINGER'S THEORY

Karl Menninger, born in 1893, built his suicide theory on that of Freud. The three main components of Menninger's theory—a wish to kill, a wish to be killed, and a wish to die—were mentioned in connection with the homicidal-suicidal pattern described briefly on page 28. Menninger separates suicides into three categories: chronic suicide in which self-destructive behavior is seen, as in addiction, antisocial behavior, martyrdom, and psychosis; organic suicide in which the death wish is the response to a physical illness such as cancer; and focal suicide in which there is self-mutilation and/or multiple accidents. In the book *Man Against Himself*, Menninger examines and analyzes the deeper

37

motives of suicide and the three categories mentioned above. In the final section, he deals with available techniques of combating self-destruction.

HORNEY'S THEORY

Karen Horney (1885–1952) made an outstanding contribution to the field of psychotherapy and her writings include a different approach to explaining people's susceptibility to suicide. She believed that parental attitudes may cause a neurotic dependency in which the child is overcome by feelings of anxiety. When parents are indifferent to the needs of the child, provide a cold family atmosphere, set excessively high standards, or are constantly critical, a child may develop neurotic dependencies characterized by feelings of uneasiness, dread, and impending disaster (basic anxiety). Insecure in a hostile world, the child feels isolated and helpless. Feelings of hostility develop which become so powerful that they cannot be expressed because of helplessness and guilt. The more the hostility is repressed, the more intense the basic anxiety becomes.

One of the ways in which such a child might attempt to overcome the anxiety is to turn hostile feelings inward and to withdraw into a shell to avoid being hurt. Or there may be attempts to compensate for feelings of helplessness by exerting power over others. Feelings of superiority may be substituted for those of inferiority. The child or childlike adult develops an idealized self with a need for affection and approval that can never be satisfied.

In the process of devoting energies to living up to the idealized self (which is unreal), such a person destroys relationships with other people. This could be due to an excessive need for love, an excessive need for power or possessions, or to the feeling that the individual is misunderstood by others. Horney defined these psychological abnormalities as a failure in social and emotional growth. According to her theory, suicide is the outcome of one type of failure in self-development. As in many other theories, the element of helplessness appears to play an important part.

HENDIN'S STUDIES
OF SCANDINAVIA

Dr. Herbert Hendin, a psychoanalyst, made an extensive study of the varying causes of suicide in Denmark, Sweden, and Norway. For a hundred years or more, the rate of suicide in Denmark and Sweden has been three times greater than in Norway. Why?

Dr. Hendin went to Scandinavia where he worked with professionals, patients, and others, and gathered large amounts of data before publishing his findings. He found the differences in the suicide rates to be related to child-rearing patterns.

In Norway, where the suicide rate is comparatively low, children are not required to excel in order to win their mothers' affection. Norwegian adults do not drive themselves toward success or experience self-hate if they fail in their undertakings. Children are reared to express their natural aggression. But when there is aggressive antisocial behavior, strong guilt feelings are aroused. In general, one finds suicide only when this aggression is turned inward.

In Sweden, rigid demands for superior performance are imposed on children, and self-hate is associated with failure. In Sweden, suicidal people are identified as "performance types."

In Denmark, the high rate of suicide is thought to be the result of a high degree of dependency. Here a child's dependency on the mother is encouraged far more than in the United States. Aggression is held strictly in check and a behavior pattern develops that increases the amount and length of dependency. When the time for separation from the mother finally comes, it is very difficult because the child is likely to feel intense dependency and feelings of guilt. The Danes have been described as people who are either dependent on someone or on whom someone is dependent. When something goes amiss in this relationship, suicide is a more common answer for people who are under stress than in many other countries.

Of course, the above patterns are not characteristic of every individual, but they do represent a trend. Although Hendin's methods of studying suicide have been criticized and not everyone agrees with his conclusions, this theory sheds some light on what motivates a Danish or a Swedish person to suicide and why the rate of suicide is higher in Denmark and Sweden than in Norway. And it may help in the understanding of the causes of suicide everywhere.

THE CRIMINAL
PERSONALITY THEORY

Samuel Yochelson and Stanton E. Samenow, who are famous for their research at Saint Elizabeth's Hospital, in Washington, D.C., presented an interesting theory of suicide in their famous book, *The Criminal Personality.* According to them, a criminal's thought patterns are based on alternating feelings of worthlessness and omnipotence. In their research of fifteen years, they noted that suicidal thinking occurred from time to time in the life of every criminal they encountered. At such times, the criminal sees himself or herself as worthless and considers life not worth living. The criminal not only sees his or her own life as nothing, but feels that others are aware that this is true, and that the condition will last forever.

The suicidal phase in the life of the criminal is more than a state of depression with anger turned inward. According to this theory, the criminal is angry because his or her needs are not being fulfilled, and current suffering is seen as unending. Feeling that he or she is a victim of circumstances and that there is no way out of the present intolerable situation, the criminal sees suicide as a resolution of ending the pain of lowered self-esteem and the anger that he or she vents against the outside world.

MANY THEORIES AND MANY QUESTIONS

Just a few of the theories about why people take their own lives have been mentioned in this chapter. There are many more ideas that have been developed in attempts to help answer the question, Why suicide?

No single theory is very helpful in explaining why one person resorts to suicide and another does not. Each person has a different combination of reasons, but each person probably experiences some of the following feelings: loneliness, hate, shame, guilt, fear, desire for revenge, hopelessness, helplessness, isolation from society, and more. And these feelings, along with others, probably exist in an endless variety of combinations.

The suicidal crisis appears to come most often when the victim feels no hope for the future. Even though there may be many possibilities for a better life situation, these are overlooked or denied by the individual. Suicide, rather than being a desire for death, often appears to be more a fear of living and the problems that come with it.

5

The History
of Suicide

ANCIENT EGYPT

Some of the early records of suicide come from Egypt and indicate varied attitudes toward it. One Egyptian document, dated about 2000 B.C., contains an illustration of a man who might be contemplating suicide, but historians do not agree on the subject matter. According to the interpretation of Jacques Choron, an expert in the study of suicide, the man appears to be tired of life and is trying to persuade his soul to accompany him in death. The soul, however, is afraid that the man will be denied a proper funeral because of the suicide and thus forfeit its chances of a blissful afterlife. Since the ancient Egyptians showed such great concern about life after death, it is not surprising that Choron's interpretation of the Egyptian picture includes this concern with the afterlife.

In a later reference to suicide in early Egyptian literature, a wise man bemoans the state of social decay of the times with the remark, "Death and suicide are common, and the river is filled with corpses."[10] Suicide was a fairly common fate for condemned criminals in Egypt, and history shows there was no prohibition against anyone ending his or her life that way. The most famous Egyptian suicide, of course, was Cleopatra, who, according to legend, took her life with the help of an asp, a venomous snake.

ANCIENT WARRIORS

Many people in far parts of the earth believed violent and self-inflicted death to be a passport to a better life and another world. Since death came at an early age for most of them due to diseases or injuries for which there were no adequate medical remedies, they sacrificed some of their short lives for what they believed to be a better life after death.

Ancient Gauls and early Germanic tribes are described as having no fear of suicide since they believed that being killed in battle or taking one's life ensured happiness in the next world. Valhalla, the paradise of the Vikings, was the hall of those who died in violence. There, according to legend, a feast of the heroes was presided over by the god Odin, and only those who died violently could take part. While the greatest honor was death in battle, suicide was the second greatest qualification. Odin is said to have died in a ritual suicide. Many men and animals were later hanged on trees in his honor in the holy grove of Uppsala.

PRIMITIVE SOCIETIES

Some African tribes once followed a common custom in which warriors and slaves committed suicide when

43

the tribal king died. They believed if they died this way they would be with their king in paradise.

In many primitive hunting and gathering societies, suicide was common because death was preferable to a life of infirmity, although this was not true everywhere. Anthropologists and others believe suicide was completely unknown in some primitive tribes.

In many societies where personal fulfillment is less important than the well-being of the masses, both good and bad situations are accepted as part of the natural order of things. In such societies, there was and is less stress-related suicide. If good and evil spirits are responsible for the highs and lows in a person's life, then one does not have to suffer from guilt. Today may be controlled by evil spirits, but tomorrow may be different. So there is always hope that the good will come again, hence less suicide.

In many primitive cultures, suicide was used as an expression of anger and revenge for highly personal motives. In some of the South Sea Islands, suicide is still considered an honorable act.

Imagine the man who was accused by another tribal member of breaking a tribal taboo. He has climbed to the top of a palm tree and declared to the tribe the name of his accuser, then plunged to his death, diving head first toward the ground. This type of suicide—as an act of revenge—may have been used to accomplish the destruction of his personal enemy, even if it destroyed the person seeking the revenge. (This is also true in modern times in the case of the people who commit suicide because they want parents or other loved ones to suffer.) In some primitive tribes, there is also the belief that the ghost of the dead person will destroy the offender, or his family will do so. In some cases, the laws of the tribe demand that the offender commit suicide, too.

44

SUICIDE BY WIVES

In some societies of long ago, suicide was acceptable when there were "good" reasons. Those reasons hardly would be considered valid in modern times in the Western world. For example, in the Fiji Islands immediately after a tribal chief died his wives rushed to kill themselves, believing that the one who died first would be the chieftain's favorite wife in the spirit world.

Suttee, the ancient Hindu custom, was practiced for a different reason. Here, the wife threw herself on the funeral pyre, or drowned herself in the Ganges, to atone for her husband's sins and open the gates of paradise for him. This practice, which lasted for hundreds of years, was outlawed in 1829.

GREEK AND ROMAN
ATTITUDES

Greek and Roman attitudes toward suicide varied according to time and place. In one place, there might be legal approval plus the supplying of the poison hemlock for suicide for a person who was suffering from extreme physical or mental anguish. In another place, a magistrate might condone a suicide if the person had what were considered to be admirable reasons, such as avoiding dishonor, patriotic principles, or great grief. However, there was a time in Athens when the body of someone who had committed suicide was buried outside the city limits. The hand of the body was buried separately because it had committed the crime of self-murder.

Drinking poison hemlock is famous as the method of suicide used by Socrates, the Greek philosopher and teacher of Plato. He was more or less forced by the state to die. Reports vary, but he seems to have supported the general philosophy that suicide was wrong except when there were special reasons, such as being ordered by the state, extreme cases of sorrow or poverty, or when one was in disgrace.

Stoics considered suicide as a natural solution to intolerable conditions of life and their philosophy had much influence in the Greek and Roman worlds. Stoics did not feel that suicide was morally right or wrong, but they considered it a reasonable way to end severe, but only severe, suffering.

In Rome, suicide was often regarded in an economic light, especially where soldiers and slaves were concerned. A soldier who killed himself depleted the power of the army, and a slave who committed suicide was an economic loss to the owner. Slaves represented an investment and were sold with a guarantee against physical blemishes, criminal impulses, or a suicidal nature. If a slave committed suicide within six months after purchase, his or her body could be returned to the seller.

In Rome suicide that was committed to honor country or defend a cause was considered acceptable. Many Roman nobles took their own lives with great dignity and style rather than suffer the dishonor of punishment.

Suicide became quite common in ancient Rome and this type of death was often public and even casual. People in ancient times did not view death with the horror or fear that they do today, and there were many instances of people being killed for the amusement of others. People are even reported to have offered themselves for execution for a sum of money which was to be paid to their heirs. With the decline of the Roman Empire, attitudes toward suicide changed.

HEBREW ATTITUDES

Hebrew prohibitions against suicide go back to the times when the early Egyptians condoned it, to at least two thousand years before the time of Christ. Since Hebrew fundamentalists believe God owns everything, it follows that one's body belongs to Him. But there have been cases in which heroic suicides have been condoned.

Many Jews throughout history preferred to die as martyrs rather than renounce their religion or lose their freedom.

For example, in the fortress of Masada on the edge of the desert of Judea which overlooks the Dead Sea, ancient Hebrews carried out a plan of mass suicide. They chose to free themselves by death rather than become Roman slaves. Reports of how the suicide was carried out vary, but there is little question that this was a heroic mass suicide. If you visit Israel today, you can see this historic site.

In later years, there were many suicides in Nazi concentration camps by people who were waiting to be slaughtered. This may have been an affirmation of the victims' freedom to control their own lives through fixing the time of their death. Some who escaped death in the camps later committed suicide because of the extreme guilt they felt for having survived while others died.

CHRISTIAN ATTITUDES

Many early Christians submitted to Roman torture and allowed themselves to be killed as martyrs for their religion. Other suicides from this period, whether direct or indirect, were based on the eagerness to do away with the misery of the world in order to experience the joys of immortality. In the fourth

47

century A.D., Saint Augustine spoke out against suicide and the attitude of Christians changed. From then on, suicide was considered a sin on the basis that it was self-murder and in violation of the commandment "Thou shalt not kill."

Through the years, however, attitudes continued to change. John Donne, the English poet (1573–1631), wrote *Biothanatos*, in which he launched the first full-scale attack against the attitude of the Christian church. He made a plea for charity and understanding. His book, which his son published after Donne's death, revealed that he had contemplated suicide when he was young. Later theologians were less strict about considering suicide as a sin under all circumstances. Although some Christian views today reflect the early thinking about suicide, funeral rites for suicides are often conducted on the assumption that the person was not able to think rationally and was not responsible for the act.

JAPANESE ATTITUDES

Attitudes and customs in Japan have undergone extensive and rapid change within the last few decades. While hara-kiri was forbidden by law as long ago as 1868, it continued to influence later suicides. Hara-kiri, literally translated as "stomach cutting," is done by disembowelment in a solemn and elaborate ceremony. Young boys of the military class were trained from earliest years that they might some day be called upon to play a part in the seppuku (hara-kiri) ceremony, and this early training is believed to have robbed the practice of some of its horrors. Such ceremonial death was honorable for members of the samurai, or military, class. If a samurai warrior fell into disgrace, hara-kiri would blot out the disgrace. Or, the ceremony might be performed to show one's alle-

48

giance to a chief. The helper in the ceremony was often a best friend whose function was to assist by cutting off the person's head immediately after the suicide ritual was completed. The decapitation was an act of mercy which prevented long suffering before death.

The kamikaze pilots who hurtled their planes against enemy warships ended their lives in a different manner but they, too, died in a heroic, ritual suicide. Near the end of World War II, a number of Japanese military leaders committed hara-kiri rather than accept surrender.

The old attitudes toward suicide of the honored and military class probably played a part in the rate of suicide in Japan for a long time. The famous Japanese author Yukio Mishima took his life in 1970 as a plea for the return of old values, but many of the young Japanese were not impressed. Mishima proclaimed the values of the samurai, invaded the headquarters of the Japanese Self-Defense Force, and committed seppuku, the time-honored ritualistic suicide by disembowelment. The initial reaction was to declare him insane and fanatical, but the day after his death, the Japanese people were asked to respect his motives and he was described as a martyr. Some writers continue to condone suicide as an acceptable means of dealing with harsh and difficult problems. However, there are many new attitudes.

At one time, women in Japan were educated to be dominated by parents, husband, husband's parents, and even by male children. They felt rejected if they were not chosen to be someone's wife, for they had little hope of financial security. Along with this hopelessness came a high rate of suicide for women.

Even as Japan became modernized, men came in growing numbers from remote provinces to the cities. Their conservative conception of femininity strongly influenced urban attitudes, which had become more liberal. In merchant districts, where women had a higher status. this provided increasing role conflicts for young Japanese women for a time. However, today, many single women in Japan are enjoying careers, and many Japanese housewives work outside the home. The role of women has grown to be more equal with men, and the number of suicides among both single and married women has declined.

Japan's adolescent suicide rate is still one of the highest in the world. Pressure to do well in school is a cause of suicide in many cultures, but it is especially intense in Japan. Even very young children suffer from strong parental pressure for good work in school since competition is great. Being admitted to a good university usually means future security and comfort for males and a better marriage for females. Since suicide can be called aggression turned inward, it may not surprise us to find a great number of suicides in a country such as Japan where overt expressions of anger toward authority figures are frowned upon. But most Japanese young people do not use suicide as a way to express anger and guilt for having failed. They find culturally acceptable ways to express their feelings.

IN THE UNITED STATES

The right to die is a much debated question in the United States today. Even those who treat suicidal persons do not always agree about the right to commit suicide. Although the attitude that suicide is a sin and a crime lost favor as early as the middle of the eighteenth century, some threads of it remain. American attitudes toward suicide are described in the next chapter.

6
The Ethics
of Suicide

Attitudes about suicide have ranged from condemning people to death for trying to take their own lives to defending the rights of individuals to control their bodies no matter what the circumstances.

Most mental health professionals make every effort to prevent suicides. They emphasize the fact that how one thinks is greatly influenced by how one feels. Even pain passes. The "decision" to commit suicide can be postponed until treatment for a condition has been completed. Some individuals need to be hospitalized, even against their will, in order to protect them from harming themselves.

Consider the case of Rick, who is poised and ready to leap from the ledge of a tenth-story window. Do you feel that someone should try to stop him? Does he have the right to take his own life? Would he really want to do this if he lived another twenty-four hours?

Suicidal people often feel ambivalent, and the overwhelming impulse to end life may be transitory. It may be a momentary feeling, or it may last a few hours or days. Although suicidal feelings may linger or recur, the immediate wish to die may be overcome if the person can be given help at the time of the crisis.

Consider sixteen-year-old Sarah, single and pregnant, abandoned by the boyfriend with whom she had been living since her mother and stepfather kicked her out of their apartment. She had no money and no job, and she was desperate. After drinking a few beers one night, she became very depressed and ran out to the street into the oncoming traffic. The police were summoned, and they took her to the hospital, where she received therapy for her depression and assistance in dealing with her problems. After two weeks, she was no longer feeling hopeless and helpless. She decided that she really wanted to continue living.

Most people would probably agree that both Rick and Sarah deserved a chance to reconsider their decision to commit suicide. According to psychiatrist Dr. Jerome A. Motto of the University of California School of Medicine in San Francisco, suicidal impulses may emerge in people who suffer severe physical or emotional pain. Suicide is a way of coping with that pain. Dr. Motto thinks that the problem is not whether the patient has the right to suicide; the dilemma stems from the philosophical position that he or she does have such a right. To what extent should the exercise of that right be subject to limitations?

While a person may have a right to suicide, is the act based on a realistic assessment of his or her life situation or on a gross distortion? When people are suicidal, they often have a warped view of their lives. A person who feels unworthy, unloved, and isolated from other human beings may develop a new and more realistic perspective through therapy.

But is there such a concept as rational suicide? Some experts in the fields of ethics and medicine have argued that sometimes suicide is rationally justified.

Dr. Glenn C. Graber, a professor of philosophy at

the University of Tennessee, cites the example of a secret agent who is captured by the enemy in wartime. He knows that he will be tortured to death, so he bites a cyanide capsule and dies. According to Dr. Graber, suicide is the only rational option in this situation, since the choice is between immediate death or death in the very near future. The agent is aware that this enemy never spares captured spies, so by killing himself he avoids a more painful death, as well as the possibility of divulging secret information under torture.

The concept of rational suicide has gained some acceptance, according to Dr. Seymour Perlin, professor of psychiatry at George Washington University School of Medicine and founder of the American Association of Suicidology. Many older people commit suicide, not because they are depressed but because they do not wish to go on living. Increasing numbers of elderly couples are making suicide pacts. Although people are living longer, the quality of their lives may not be very good. Studies have revealed that the suicide rate among those who are sixty-five or older increased during the 1980s (see graph on page 54). White males sixty-five and over had the highest rate of suicide, almost four times the national average, according to a study reported by the National Center for Health Statistics.[11] However, this may be an underestimate, because some deaths are not reported as suicides. Older people sometimes use less obvious means of ending their lives, such as deliberately starving themselves or discontinuing crucial medications.

Dr. S. was a seventy-five-year-old professor and distinguished scholar who suffered from terminal cancer. He shot and killed himself. Many years before, he had told his wife that if he was faced with a hopeless disease, he would commit suicide in order to spare himself and his family needless suffering. Some peo-

53

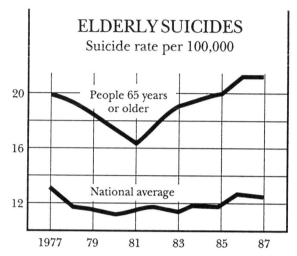

ELDERLY SUICIDES
Suicide rate per 100,000

People 65 years or older

National average

1977 79 81 83 85 87

Source: National Center for Health Statistics;
John L. McIntosh, Indiana University

ple would agree that this was rational suicide, but others feel that any form of suicide is wrong.

Chris was a young man terminally ill with AIDS. He was weak, blind, and wracked with pain; he suffered from constant infections that could no longer be checked by medication. Finally, he asked his doctor to discontinue any further treatment; he wanted only to be kept as comfortable as possible, with pain-killing medication and good nursing care. He also requested that no one try to save his life by heroic measures. For instance, if he stopped breathing, he did not want to be resuscitated and connected to a machine that would pump air into his lungs. Chris developed severe pneumonia, but in accordance with his wishes, the doctors did not give him medication or oxygen. He rapidly slipped into unconsciousness and died peacefully two days later.

Do you think that this was suicide? Did the doctors help Chris commit suicide? Or did the doctors actually commit murder by not treating Chris?

David was a thirty-eight-year-old quadriplegic who had been paralyzed seventeen years earlier in a surfing accident, and he was totally helpless, unable to move or breathe on his own. His parents were dead and he had no close friends living nearby. He became increasingly discouraged and bitter; his existence was so barren that he felt he was already dead. So he requested that his respirator be disconnected. A judge in a Michigan court agreed that he had the right to refuse treatment. A few weeks later, surrounded by a few friends, David drifted into sleep after being given a sedative by his physician. His respirator was removed, and he died peacefully within an hour.

Do you think that this was a rational suicide? David did not have a terminal illness and might have lived another twenty years.

In earlier times, death and dying were much less complicated. There were no antibiotics to cure infections and no respiratory machines to keep people breathing. The definition of death was simple: when a person stopped breathing or when the heart stopped beating, the person was diagnosed as dead. But with advances in technology, death had to be redefined. The invention of the heart-lung machine meant that a person could be kept alive indefinitely, even if the brain had been destroyed. By 1990, most states had changed the definition of death to include irreversible cessation of all brain function.

Traditionally, physicians have been morally obligated to treat disease and use every means available to preserve life. But there have been changes in the way people think about this issue. The assertion that life should be preserved at all costs has been challenged by many, including health care professionals, ethicists, clergy, and lawmakers. Increasing numbers of people believe that there is no moral or ethical obligation to preserve life when recovery is not possible and when life becomes too burdensome. Several polls have shown that a large majority of Americans believe that people should have the right to refuse treatment, and they approve of discontinuing treatment in hopeless cases. In such cases, the intention is not death but the relief from suffering. A death resulting from discontinuing treatment would not be considered suicide or homicide, but rather a consequence of the disease itself. According to the law, an adult who is mentally competent has the right to refuse treatment, even if that decision results in death. For instance, a person who opposes the use of blood transfusions on religious grounds cannot be forced to accept a transfusion which might mean the difference between life and death.

As of the end of 1989, forty states and the District of Columbia had passed right-to-die or "living will" laws. A living will is a legal document that enables an individual to state in advance specific wishes about his or her treatment in case of terminal illness.

Despite living will laws and numerous court decisions affirming the rights of people to discontinue treatment, there is still confusion and controversy. Many such cases are decided by the courts because some doctors and hospitals are afraid of being sued or prosecuted if they discontinue treatment or "pull the plug," even when the patient and family members all agree. In order to make sure that patients' rights are protected, hospital ethics committees set up guidelines and review these difficult cases. Experts believe that it has become crucial for all health care institutions to develop policies concerning the use and removal of life-sustaining treatment. Many people

56

would agree that "pulling the plug" when the situation is hopeless is not murder, suicide, or assisted suicide.

Assisted suicide is a subject that was rarely discussed publicly in the past. Many people who are terminally ill ask their doctors to help them die, and many doctors have quietly given them help, even though assisted suicide is illegal in the United States. However, recently the debate has become more open. Medical advances enable people to live longer, but many are very dissatisfied with the quality of their lives. As noted earlier, suicide among the elderly is increasing, possibly as a result of this dissatisfaction. The devastating effects of AIDS in its terminal stages has also given rise to numerous suicides. Among people with AIDS, suicide is often openly discussed as a way of gaining some control over death. Many AIDS patients hoard medications so that they can commit suicide by taking an overdose. No one knows how many physicians have prescribed drugs that they knew would be used for this purpose.

The Hemlock Society is an organization that supports the right of terminally ill individuals to take their own lives. Recently, they have also been active in advocating changes in the law that would allow physician-assisted suicide. A proposed "Death with Dignity" act failed to qualify for the ballot in California in 1988, but the Hemlock Society and other groups are campaigning for referenda there and in other states in the early 1990s. According to one poll, 64 percent of those surveyed thought that assisted suicide for the terminally ill should be legalized.[12]

Mercy killing in Holland has been debated more publicly and performed more openly than in any other country. For a long time, although mercy killing has been illegal, Dutch physicians have been assisting patients to die, using strict criteria. The patient must be suffering unbearable pain and must have a clear mind; the request must be made voluntarily and over a period of time. Physicians who have performed mercy killing in Holland have rarely been prosecuted, and in 1984 the highest court ruled that a physician could not be convicted of a crime if he or she acted out of professional duty to a patient.

Euthanasia is another term that is used for mercy killing, although it means simply "good death." There is a difference between passive euthanasia (allowing someone to die) and active euthanasia (intentional killing). Despite the number of people in Holland and other countries around the world who approve of active euthanasia under certain circumstances, there are many others who are vehemently opposed.

In June 1990, a sensational case of physician-assisted suicide stirred up renewed controversy over the right-to-die issue. Dr. Jack Kevorkian, a retired pathologist, connected a woman with Alzheimer's disease to a homemade suicide machine at her request. (After she pushed a button, allowing poison to flow into her bloodstream, she died.) Dr. Kevorkian's actions were considered immoral by many, but this case emphasizes the need to come to grips with the problem of euthanasia.

Referring to what is known as the "slippery slope" argument, some fear that even voluntary passive euthanasia could lead society into a downward slide toward intentional killing of others such as the handicapped and the mentally retarded. Active euthanasia has been compared to the Nazi program of eliminating people whom the German government judged undesirable or useless.

There are many questions concerning an individual's right to commit suicide. The issue of assisted

58

suicide brings up further troublesome dilemmas and hot debate. But there are many opinions and no simple answers in this continuing controversy over the right to die.

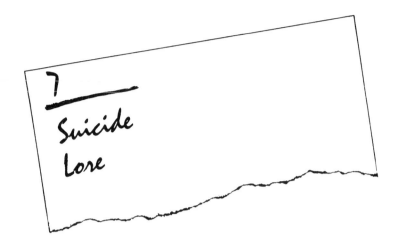

7

Suicide Lore

Suppose one of your friends confides in you that he or she is going to commit suicide. What would you do? What would you say? You might suggest that the friend think of more pleasant things. You might laugh about the remark, hoping that the threat was a joke. You might think that the person is using this threat as a way of getting attention or of manipulating you to do something that you did not plan to do. You might even ignore the remark because you have heard that people who talk about committing suicide never do.

The idea that people who talk about suicide never take their lives is a dangerous fallacy and one of the most popular parts of the great body of suicide lore. If a friend confides in you that he or she is going to commit suicide, one of the best things you can do is to know the difference between fallacies and truths and act immediately. How to act is described in a later chapter. First, here are some popular fallacies that lead people to wrong responses.

60

"PEOPLE WHO TALK ABOUT SUICIDE DON'T TAKE THEIR LIVES"

Verbal expressions such as "I might as well be dead" or "You'll be better off without me" are chief among the danger signals or clues given by people who eventually commit suicide. Of 134 families interviewed in a study to determine suicidal communication, it was discovered that 41 percent of the victims had specifically stated their intent to commit suicide. Many investigators report a wide range of verbal clues recalled by families of people who have taken their lives. Since such clues are things most families of victims do not want to remember, it may be that far more victims have given verbal hints about their intentions. Families of suicidal people frequently suffer from feelings of guilt and may forget such statements. Many studies indicate that as many as 60 to 80 percent of the persons who commit suicide had communicated their intentions before they died.

"ALL PEOPLE WHO COMMIT SUICIDE ARE CRAZY"

"Crazy" and "insane" are words we all use, applied mostly to people who behave in ways that seem strange to us. They are also used to label those who are suffering from serious emotional illnesses that affect their thinking and behavior. Psychiatrists may use the term "psychotic" to denote a great loss in a person's ability to evaluate his or her perceptions correctly. For example, if an individual thinks that he is receiving messages through his television set, he would be considered to have impaired reality testing.

Psychosis may be caused by schizophrenia, drug abuse, alcohol abuse, or other disorders. Some people

61

who are suffering from psychotic disorders may take their lives because their thinking and judgment are severely distorted. For example, a schizophrenic woman heard her dead mother calling, so she overdosed on sleeping pills in order to join her mother in heaven. A depressed man set himself on fire because he was obeying the commands of the devils who possessed him.

Certainly, the idea that all people who commit suicide are crazy is a myth. Psychological analysis of youth suicides indicate that about half of them had a relatively recent contact with the mental health system, but this included people who were seeing counselors and various therapists for a variety of problems. Drug use was prominent in the study, as well as conduct disorders and major stress events, such as the loss of a parent through suicide.

"IMPROVEMENT OF A SUICIDAL PATIENT MEANS THE DANGER IS OVER"

Most schizophrenics do not ordinarily commit suicide in response to hallucinations or panic, but those who take their own lives do so because they are unable to adapt when they are in an improved state. In cases of depressive illness, suicide is more likely to occur when the person is improving. S. A. Applebaum has described suicide as a problem-solving technique to "save the integrity of the psychological system despite its catastrophic effects in other respects."[13]

Even after an unsuccessful suicide attempt, one must continue to assess the risk of another attempt. Most suicides occur within three months after the beginning of improvement. The act of suicide usually involves some planning and activity. People who are severely depressed frequently suffer from inertia.

When they begin to improve, they have more energy which can be used to put morbid thoughts and feelings into action. It may also be true that improvement is only on the surface, while deep inside the suicidal people are not really better. Certain people grow calm and appear happy just before suicide because they are no longer in conflict over whether or not to live.

"SUICIDE IS A DISEASE"

Avery D. Weisman made a study at Massachusetts General Hospital, in Boston, on the subject of suicide as a disease.[14] He concluded that suicide is neither a moral dilemma nor a mental disease, but a form of life-threatening behavior which resembles a declaration of war. There is no evidence of organic disease to explain it, and while disease involves sickness, sickness does not always involve disease. Weisman found that suicide might be an attempt to break through one's indecision about living and dying, but unfortunately, one may die of the side effects.

Rather than considering suicide as a disease, a crisis, or a conflict, Weisman decided that the sickness of suicide might better be thought of as "lethality." This concept, attributed to the suicidologist Edwin Shneidman, may be broadly defined as the disposition to kill oneself or put one's life in danger. Suicidologists consider lethality as a very helpful concept.

The following case, which illustrates a lethal but no longer suicidal situation, may help to show how these words are used by experts. For several weeks, Ms. X had considered suicide because of family problems that she believed were insurmountable. One day she wrote a suicide note, then she got into her car and drove to a high bridge for a rehearsal of her suicide plans. On the morning of her attempt, she went about her household chores as usual, then drove to the bridge. After parking her car, she climbed over the railing and paused, ready to leap. Again, as she had many times during the past few weeks, she grew undecided about whether or not to end her life. She considered the stigma on her children that would result from her act, but she felt that killing herself was a form of revenge upon her husband. Ms. X believed that people who jumped from high places died before they reached the ground or the water and she expected this to happen to her. She let go of the railing as a way of overcoming her indecision, and fell toward the water. On the way down, she realized she was not dead and wished that she would be rescued. This is known because she *was* rescued by a fisherman who happened to be nearby. After reaching the hospital, she was no longer suicidal; her feelings had changed. No one who helped her while she recovered from her fractures could determine why she suffered from the desire to take her life before her suicide attempt. Conditions at home were no better when she returned but she had broken through her lethality. The suicide attempt may have been partially motivated by guilt and was her way of punishing herself for her imagined faults. In this way she atoned, and thus alleviated her guilt.

Some suicidologists think that the significance of attempting suicide is its use in overcoming the quandary of not being able to choose whether to live or die. The attempt at suicide may be the way used to break through the lethality. Unfortunately, in successful attempts, the cure results in death.

"THE CHANCES OF SUICIDE CAN BE REDUCED BY AVOIDING THE SUBJECT"

Actually, one can reduce the chances of suicide by bringing the subject into the open. If a boy suggests that he might kill himself and you respond by saying,

"You wouldn't do anything that stupid," you are confirming his already low opinion of himself. He feels more alone, he feels wrong, and he feels even less acceptable than he did before he made the remark that was actually a cry for help.

Since what you say to a suicidal person may play a large part in the life or death of another person, you can see how important it is to know what to say or what not to say. Knowing not to treat suicide as a taboo subject is one of the first steps toward prevention.

The old attitude of hiding or denying suicide has been the cause of many unnecessary deaths. Here is a case in point. A doctor who was treating a young boy for depression and who found him to be suicidal recommended that the boy be hospitalized. He found that the boy's father was cooperative, but the mother would not consider such a thing. What would the neighbors think? She refused to accept the idea that the boy might take his life.

One afternoon, the boy sat in a rented hotel room for three hours with a pistol pointed at his head. Then he put the pistol in his pocket and returned home. Even after the therapist revealed this event to the father, the parents would not consider hospitalization. A few weeks later, the boy threatened to punish his mother for always nagging at him. He hanged himself in the basement while she was getting dinner.

Now, the mother was furious with the doctor for not warning of the possibility of suicide. Both parents visited the doctor and reproached him with angry words and threats. When in the presence of the mother, the father denied ever having been warned of the possibility of suicide. Perhaps they would have to live with feelings of guilt and the stigma of suicide for the rest of their lives. Was this stigma a major part of their grief? How different this case might have been if the parents could have accepted the boy's behavior without their personal concern for the attitudes of others!

Talking about suicide with a person who is trained to help can often minimize the anxiety that goes with this kind of thinking and may prevent the action from taking place. If you recognize a clue that someone is contemplating suicide, pick up the phone and get a suicide-prevention center or other emergency center (see Appendix) to help him or her.

"SUICIDAL PERSONS AVOID MEDICAL HELP"

A common misconception about suicidal persons is that they shy away from medical help. Studies on the backgrounds of people who have committed suicide show that as many as 60 to 70 percent had sought medical help within six months before the suicide. Eight out of ten suicides give some warning. No one knows exactly how many gave clues to the doctors about their suicide plans, but doctors are becoming more alert to suicidal intent and taking action that can help prevent suicide. The relationship between physical and emotional health is recognized in the work of an increasing number of professionals.

"THERE IS A TYPE OF PERSON WHO COMMITS SUICIDE"

"She was not the type."

"Only the rich commit suicide."

"No wonder he took his life. Suicide is the curse of the poor."

There is no "type" where suicide is concerned. All kinds of people end their own lives. Male and female; young, old, and all the ages in between; rich, poor, and middle-income people; people of all shades

66

of skin; manic and depressive; mentally ill and mentally healthy; these are all people who have been suicidal. Anyone might be.

So often one hears the statement, "He just wasn't the type," soon after a suicide. Knowing that there is no one type, that any person may be vulnerable, may make it easier to recognize clues and prevent the tragic waste of lives through suicide.

"SUICIDE ATTEMPTS ARE SELDOM REPEATED"

The truth is that once a person tries death by suicide he or she is very likely to make another attempt. Some people make many attempts and continue until they are finally successful. Thirty to 40 percent of those who complete suicide have made previous attempts.

In determining the risk of suicide, one of the important factors is whether or not the person has attempted suicide before. However, since the suicidal mood is usually a temporary one, a great many people who attempt suicide are diverted from this kind of action and never try again. Even those who try several times may resolve their problems in more positive ways and go on to lead rewarding lives.

"NOTHING CAN BE DONE ABOUT SUICIDE"

In spite of modern attitudes, many people believe that nothing can be done about suicide. Certainly there are cases where suicide attempts have been stopped and the person commits suicide at a later date. No statistics can ever be available for the actual number of suicides that have been prevented by calls to suicide-prevention centers, but there are hundreds of these centers functioning and an untold number of people who are alive today because of them.

"SUICIDE IS A SPONTANEOUS ACT. IT HAPPENS WITHOUT WARNING"

Most suicidal people fantasize or plan their self-destruction long before making the attempt. They give numerous clues and warnings, as mentioned elsewhere in this book. It should be pointed out that when suicides are prevented the majority of people never try it again. They go on to lead full and happier lives, never giving suicide even a passing thought.

"TELLING PEOPLE TO CHEER UP WILL HELP THEM"

When a child or adolescent is considering suicide, being told to cheer up only makes him or her feel worse. If people knew the pain, they would understand that it is impossible to "cheer up." Moods will change and bad situations may improve tomorrow, but many children cannot look much beyond the present.

Telling a suicidal person what a good life he or she has, or how much better that person is than some others, only increases the depression and adds to the guilt. Even one who can intellectualize about the good things may not be able to believe in them. There just is no good life in the minds of those who want to die. People who say "cheer up" are not listening to the cry for help.

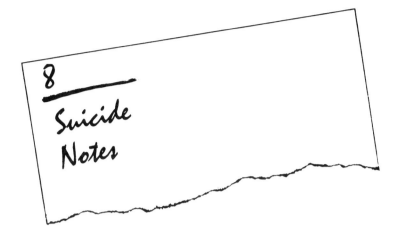

8
Suicide
Notes

At first glance, suicide notes might be considered windows into the minds of people who are about to commit suicide. Statistics telling what percentage of people leave notes vary from 15 percent to 25 percent, but large numbers of notes do exist. How such notes are interpreted varies a great deal, too.

Certainly, in most cases suicide appears to be a dramatic detail in a series of circumstances, but the suicide notes are almost always written just before the act. This appears to be one of the reasons that the notes are disappointing to those who hope they will provide insight into the past characteristics of the person. Such notes normally do not expose the real causes of the suicide, even if they do identify the precipitating event.

One famous suicide note that gave some information about the feelings and reasons for suicide was that written by Virginia Woolf to her husband, Leonard. The celebrated British novelist committed suicide by drowning in 1941. The note read:
I feel certain I am going mad again. . . . And I shan't

69

recover this time. I begin to hear voices, and I can't concentrate. . . . I can't fight any longer. . . . What I want to say is I owe all the happiness of my life to you. I can't go on spoiling your life any longer.

TYPICAL EXPRESSIONS
IN SUICIDE NOTES

Suicide notes have contained such sentences as: "I am in pain," "I am sorry," "I hate to let you down, this way is best," "Take care of our son and daughter," "Children, be good to your mother [or father]," "You drove me to this," "The car engine needs tuning," "Give Tom the $150 which I owe him," "I hope this is what you wanted," "Be sure to feed my cat."

These messages show some of the things that seem important to people in the final moments of life. Many notes contain just a few sentences. Hostility is often expressed in a disguised way. For example, a note that says, "I'm no good. Mary deserves much better," sounds humble but it may really express hidden hostility. The underlying meaning may be, "Mary makes me feel I'm no good. She thinks she deserves better." While the person may be aware only of the unhappiness that he or she feels, the element of aggressiveness or hostility is frequently expressed. "Mary, I hate you, Love, John" is not uncommon in its combination of sentiments.

Apologies for causing trouble, directions for disposing of one's body, expressions that beg forgiveness, information that indicates the person has given clues of intentions which were ignored are all common elements in notes. Apologies are typical in cases of feelings of low self-esteem, and low esteem is typical in suicidal people. It is not surprising to find notes that include such expressions. One rather famous note was written by a workman who chalked the following on the outside of an abandoned house before hanging himself. He wrote: "Sorry about this. There's a corpse in here. Inform police."

While most suicide notes are found near the body of the writer, a few find their way into newspaper columns that give personal advice. Recently, a writer began a letter to a columnist with an announcement that "this is a suicide note." Then the person, who signed it "No Name, No City, But I've Got Counterparts All Over," proceeded to tell the columnist that she would probably have the same reaction about suicide as most people and stop reading at the beginning of the note. Of course, if the writer had been truly convinced that it was futile to expect help, he or she probably would not have taken the trouble to write.

TUNNEL VISION

People who are about to take their lives are believed to suffer from a condition known as tunnel vision. This is a state in which a person's perception is narrowed and only one alternative, suicide, seems to be the way to cope with problems. In other words, the crisis situation precludes the awareness of other ways to change a situation and stops the person from pursuing a course that will lead out of this suicidal state. Feelings of hopelessness, helplessness, and emotional isolation may be increased by a person's inability to escape from what has been called the "closed world of suicide."

Tunnel vision makes it difficult for anyone to write a note with any depth. Edwin S. Shneidman, professor of thanatology at the University of California at Los Angeles and one of the world's outstanding authorities on suicide, has studied suicide notes for many years. Professor Shneidman wonders if the personal emptiness which may precede suicide might not account for the fact that suicide notes are relatively arid and psychologically barren.

REAL VERSUS SIMULATED NOTES

In *Clues to Suicide,* an investigation edited by Edwin S. Shneidman and Norman L. Farberow, there is an appendix which includes over thirty paired suicide notes. One of each pair is a genuine note and one is simulated. The actual notes were obtained from the public records of the coroner's office in Los Angeles County, California, and the simulated notes were obtained as part of an experiment. Nonsuicidal individuals were asked to write "suicide notes" of the kind they thought they would write if they were going to take their own lives. The nonsuicidal individuals who participated in the experiment were chosen to match, as nearly as possible, many characteristics of the actual note writers. The readers of *Clues to Suicide* can examine the paired notes and test themselves on their ability to distinguish the real from the simulated notes. A key is given at the end. Many people who have read the book or who are knowledgeable about suicide can easily distinguish the real notes from the false ones.

While some actual suicide notes are long, many are short and superficial. Professor Shneidman has said, in his book *Suicidology: Contemporary Developments,* that a truly suicidal person cannot write a meaningful suicide note. Conversely, if one could write a meaningful suicide note that person would not have to commit suicide. The sense of personal emptiness is often expressed as, "I can't find my place in life."

ANSWERING THE CRY FOR HELP

One suicide note begins with the remark that the stigma suicide brings upon the family "cannot be

72

more than has already been done." In some cases, the very fact that the person feels that stigma may be attached to suicide may be a way of punishing those who the suicidal person believes have treated him or her unfairly.

Even though suicidal people often feel that the stigma attached to suicide is so great that no one will want to help, the numerous suicide-prevention centers throughout the world show the opposite to be true. One interesting experiment in which a person published a suicide note for the reaction it would bring is described in *Life-Threatening Behavior*.[15] Leland Moss was a student of Professor Edwin Shneidman when this suicidologist was teaching a course in social relations at Harvard University. Mr. Moss placed an ad in the Personals column of the paper *Boston After Dark* which read:

> M 21 student gives self 3 weeks before popping pills for suicide. If you know any good reasons why I shouldn't, please write Box D-673.

The response was surprising, even to the writer of the false suicide note. Within a month, he had received 169 letters, although not all were serious replies by people who cared. Over a third of the responses were received in the first three days after the appearance of the ad. One letter, which came from as far away as Brazil, was written by a minister who was the father of a student at Massachusetts Institute of Technology. The student sent the ad to his father since he felt his father could give good advice.

While many letters told about the writers' own problems, a large number of people suggested ways of coping by developing an appreciation of nature. A large percentage of people who answered did so with

73

compassion and concern. A small group who responded questioned whether or not the ad was sincere, and one remarked, "At first I wondered if you were serious or not. . . . If it's a joke, it's in poor taste. . . ."

Such an ad would indeed have been a bad joke if it were done frivolously. But the study of responses told something about people's reactions to suicide notes.

Mr. Moss felt that a sizable number of people who replied to his ad agreed with Professor Shneidman's doctrine that all suicides might be prevented and that a cry for help should be answered as directly and swiftly as possible.

SUICIDAL THINKING PATTERNS

A number of serious studies have been made on suicide notes in efforts to discover more about what goes on in the minds of people who commit suicide. In addition to the authorities already mentioned, others such as Jerry Jacobs, Jacob Tuckman, Gene Lester, David Lester, C. Osgood, and E. G. Walker have analyzed genuine suicide notes and compared them with counterfeit notes. They found that, in general, the real suicide notes contained more words such as "maybe," "but," and "except," indicating that there was increased vacillation in the thinking of suicidal people. Osgood and Walker found a greater number of verbs dealing with simple action in the true notes than in the false ones, and a less frequent use of verbs that dealt with planning and judgment. True notes included many terms of endearment. The studies indicated that one of the hallmarks of suicidal thinking was the inability to reflect on or think through the implications of their thoughts. Conclusions from these and other studies of suicide notes are that people about to commit suicide are rigid, constricted, and polarized in

74

their thinking processes so that they are unable to imagine other ways to cope with problems. Some authorities describe this as an "impoverishment of internal judgment process." It might also be described simply as a type of thinking that ignores other ways out.

Studies of suicide notes may not reveal the nature and causes of suicide, but they do help in understanding the thought processes of the individual about to take his or her own life. Notes do show the pattern of thinking to be a sterile one. Except in cases of terminal illness, the situation appears to be a crisis in which intervention may prevent suicide and give hope for a better future.

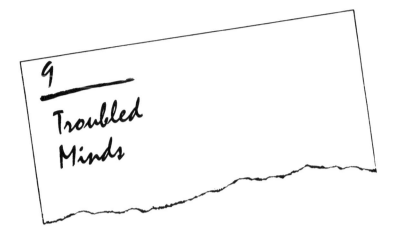

9
Troubled Minds

What are the feelings and thoughts that might lead people to kill themselves? The motivation is different for each individual, but often the forerunner of suicide is the psychic pain associated with depression and other troubled emotional states.

DEPRESSION

Recent surveys tell of an increase in the number of children and adolescents who suffer from severe types of "lows" or depression. Yale University researcher Dr. Myrna M. Weissman says the relatives of people who experienced depression when they were young are far more likely to be depressed, too. Even though it is hard to find a set of rules acceptable to psychiatrists for diagnosing childhood depression, it appears to be increasing.

Everyone has the "blues" occasionally—times when nothing seems right, and when life does not seem to be as enjoyable as usual. The reason may be a let-down feeling after an exciting vacation, a long

76

stretch of bleak weather, or a disappointing event. These are examples of a normal type of depression—a temporarily lowered mood state which does not interfere seriously with one's perception of life or one's ability to function. Most people manage to recover quickly from minor setbacks, but others stay depressed and cannot overcome their low spirits.

RECOGNIZING DEPRESSION

The risk of a depressed person committing suicide is fifty times higher than for a person who is not depressed. If you can learn to recognize the signs of depression, you may be able to save someone you know from suffering, or even from suicide.

A depressed person may exhibit any of the numerous warning signals in varying degrees. The prevailing mood is that of sadness, and the person may appear gloomy and apathetic. He or she may express feelings of emptiness and numbness, and a lack of ability to enjoy anything. His or her attitude may be hopeless and pessimistic. Feelings of worthlessness, guilt, and anxiety are common. Suicidal preoccupation is often present. There may be difficulty in concentrating or remembering things. Often, the person has trouble making decisions, even concerning unimportant matters.

Friends may notice that the individual has become withdrawn and uncommunicative, and is avoiding social activities that were formerly enjoyed. There is a decline in sexual drive. Insomnia and other changes in sleep habits are common. Many depressed people awaken very early in the morning and cannot fall asleep again. Others sleep more than usual, thus escaping, at least temporarily, from their emotional pain.

Physical symptoms such as fatigue and loss of appetite are not unusual. In fact, many people who consult physicians for physical complaints such as headaches, palpitations, back pain, and other ailments turn out to be suffering from depression in disguise, or masked depression. Underlying depression may also masquerade as an alcohol problem, compulsive overeating, or sexual promiscuity.

Depression in children and adolescents is often masked, with the result that their behavior is puzzling. When ten-year-old Robert's parents were divorced, his grades began to slip; his teacher complained that he was inattentive in class and picked fights with other children. Robert did not suddenly become a "bad" child. He was reacting to his father's absence.

Depression in children and adolescents often goes unrecognized because the symptoms are deceptive, as in the case of Robert. Other behavior, such as truancy, disobedience, and self-destructive acts may also be expressions of unrecognized depression. Sometimes adolescent depression is not noticed because it is normal for adolescents to experience some extreme fluctuations in mood.

Recent reports in medical journals show that adolescents can often suffer from the same outward and inward signs of depression that adults experience.

Dr. Carl P. Malmquist of the University of Minnesota has noted several warning signs which may be useful clues to depression in children.

1. Persistent sadness, in contrast to the temporary unhappy moods that normally occur in all children from time to time.

2. Low self-concept.

3. Provocative, aggressive behavior, or other behavior that leads people to reject or avoid the child.

4. Proneness to be disappointed easily when things do not go exactly as planned.

5. Physical complaints such as headaches, stomachaches, sleep problems, or fatigue, similar to those experienced by depressed adults.

BIOLOGICAL FACTORS

No one today believes, as the ancients thought, that depression is caused by an excess of black bile in the body. However, we know that the old theories were not totally erroneous. Scientists have discovered biochemical abnormalities in association with depressive states, and they think that these changes in body chemistry may play an important role in the development of depression, or may be the product of depression. Biochemical abnormality is only one of many variables that may be responsible for depression. There is also evidence that genetic factors may play a part in increasing a person's vulnerability to depression.

Recent studies suggest that there are lower concentrations of certain chemicals in the brains of those who attempt suicide and in some cases this is not tied to depression or other psychiatric disorders. Much more research needs to be done, but the biology of suicide is now receiving increased attention.

EXPERIENCE OF LOSS

There have been many studies that suggest there is a definite relationship between emotional loss in the young and the development of depression.

In one experiment, infant monkeys were separated from their mothers and left without any stimulation for forty-five days. When they were removed from isolation, they did not play with the other monkeys, but remained apathetic and huddled in a corner, exhibiting what appeared to be depressed behavior.

Other experiments with monkeys have demonstrated that even short periods of separation from the mother have had long-term effects such as increased clinging to the mother and arrested social development.

Human babies separated from their mothers react in similar fashion. René A. Spitz was one of the first to describe the response of babies as young as six months to the loss of their mothers. A type of depression known as hospitalism used to be seen in institutions, where children did not receive enough mothering from anyone. Even though they were well cared for and all their physical needs met, many of these children became apathetic and withdrawn. Some literally wasted away and died from lack of mothering.

The following case graphically demonstrates the effect of separation and inadequate mothering on a young child. Jimmy was one year old when his mother died suddenly. Until then, he had been a happy, bright, alert child. After his mother's death he was cared for by a succession of housekeepers, none of whom stayed more than three months. He became withdrawn, lethargic, and sad; he stopped smiling and talking. By the age of two years, he looked like a retarded child.

Animal studies and observation of young children have led to the conclusion that early loss or deprivation can make people more sensitized to loss and susceptible to depression in later life. The loss may be actual physical separation, or it may be emotional. Emotional loss may encompass a range of different kinds of emotional rejection by the people taking care of the child, from outright abuse to subtle and hidden hostility.

In adults, loss may be real, fantasized, or symbolic. Examples of real loss are the death of a parent or other loved one, loss of health due to injury or age, loss of status, loss of self-esteem or self-confidence, and loss of security. A fantasized loss involves the loss of hope of fulfilling an important goal in one's life. For instance, Bill broke his leg, thereby preventing him from competing in the Olympics. Although the injury would not prevent him from skiing again, it was severe enough so that it dashed his hopes of entering the Olympics. He took his life. Most people would not react to this misfortune by committing suicide as Bill did, because most people would not invest so much emotional energy in a single goal.

A young woman lost an inexpensive ring given to her as a child by her mother, who had died shortly afterward. She suffered a depressive reaction to the loss that was not commensurate with the actual value of the ring. It is clear that the ring had symbolic, and not real, value.

No one knows the exact relationship between loss and depression. Each individual is different, and no two people have had exactly similar life experiences. Therefore, each may react differently to the same loss. One may become mildly discouraged, another may become severely depressed, and someone else might commit suicide.

Everyone normally experiences separations and losses throughout life. It has been noted that some people seem better able to overcome loss than others; those who are unable to master these experiences are perhaps more prone to later depression.

STRESS

Investigators studying the effects of stressful life events have found that experiences of loss are high on the list of stressful situations. Dr. Eugene S. Paykel, a British psychiatrist, has analyzed the relationship between life stress, depression, and suicide. For these studies, a list of life situations that are considered stressful was compiled. Examples of some of the thirty-three events are marital separation, serious illness, death of a close family member, a move, marriage, pregnancy, leaving school, change in work, promotion, and being fired. You may be surprised to see that both desirable and undesirable events are included.

Depressed people were shown to have experienced many more of these events than the general population. While there was no significant difference in the number of desirable events, the depressive group reported a much higher incidence of undesirable events than the control group.

Events were also categorized in terms of entrances and exits, that is, the introduction of new people or the departure of familiar people from the individual's life. It was found the depressives reported more exits than did the control group. The exit or departure of an important person from one's life is a loss, and as noted earlier, loss bears an important relationship to depression.

Suicide attempters were compared with depressives and with a control group. The suicidal group reported more events in all categories, except desirable events, when compared with the control group. They experienced the same number of exits as the depressives, but reported a significantly higher number of entrances than either the depressive or the control groups.

The suicidal group was found to have experienced a greater number of events that are designated as threatening. Threatening events include major stressful situations, undesirable experiences, and

82

those situations that are not under the control of the individual. Dr. Paykel's conclusion is that suicide attempts seem to be a response to many different kinds of events, especially those in the threatening category.

When the time of occurrence was studied, it was found that depressive individuals reported a rise in the number of stressful events during the three months preceding relapse of depression. The suicidal group experienced not only a greater number of stressful events during the six months before the attempt, when compared to the general population, but also a significant peak in the month immediately prior to the attempt.

Life stress has been linked with a number of disorders, but no one knows why stress may precipitate depression in one person and suicide in another, while yet another may develop schizophrenia, and others have no significant reaction. Genetic and biological differences, in addition to other unknowns, all play a role in determining the individual's reaction to stress.

HELPLESSNESS, HOPELESSNESS, AND EMOTIONAL ISOLATION

Emotional loss early in life means more than loss of love; it involves the lack of opportunity to interact and elicit responses from a caring person. According to some experts, individuals who discover early in life that no one responds to their needs learn to view themselves as helpless. This learned helplessness may be a significant forerunner of depression. Those who grow up feeling that nothing they say or do has much impact on the world around them are likely to conclude that they have little control over their lives. They begin to see themselves as ineffective and may develop a negative self-image. This negative view leads them to believe that they are more helpless and less competent than they actually are. People who have these kinds of feelings are probably more prone to depression and perhaps more likely to be susceptible to stress in the form of uncontrollable events.

Many researchers have emphasized the importance of feelings of hopelessness as part of depression. In a study of the attitudes of prisoners, investigators found that some prisoners were apathetic and depressed, while others, with equally long sentences, were relatively happy, productive, and interested in many things. Their attitudes were not dependent on the length of sentence, the kind of job they held, or on their treatment by the guards. Their state of mind seemed to be correlated instead with their attitudes about the past and the future. Those who did "hard time" felt pessimistic and hopeless; they had no families or friends outside, no job prospects, did not believe they would be paroled, and thought their sentences were unjust. On the other hand, those who were doing "good time" had a more hopeful and optimistic attitude toward life; they thought their sentences were just, they expected parole, and they had relatives and friends outside. The hopeless, helpless, and emotionally isolated prisoners became depressed, while the others who had a more positive view of life were able to adjust to their unpleasant situation and make the best of it.

Hopelessness has been singled out as a tell-tale sign of high risk among people who are thinking about suicide. In 1985, a team under the direction of Dr. Aaron Beck reported the results of a study in the *American Journal of Psychiatry* that tried to help caretakers identify people who are at high risk. The team studied 207 patients who had been hospitalized because of intentions to commit suicide. These patients were observed over a period of from five to ten years. Checks with family and friends, scanning of daily death notices, and, in some instances, following the patients' moves to foreign countries helped the researchers. They found that a high score on the hopelessness test (below) indicated the need for careful observation of a person under treatment for years after leaving psychiatric care. Of the handful who did eventually kill themselves, no predictor, such as a test, forecast their end.

The "hopelessness scale" contains twenty statements which are scored true or false. People who have a very pessimistic view of the future are likely to get a high score, indicating a high intensity of hopeless feelings, as you can see from the scale on the following page.

Not everyone who scores high on the hopelessness test will commit suicide; in fact, the overwhelming majority of the patients with a high score did not commit suicide. The scale is, however, an instrument to estimate suicidal risk. The more we learn about the exact relationship between hopelessness and ultimate suicide, the greater the optimism that suicide can be predicted and prevented.

THE HOPELESSNESS SCALE[16]

Key	Item
True	2. I might as well give up because I can't make things better for myself.
	4. I can't imagine what my life would be like in 10 years.
	7. My future seems dark to me.
	9. I just don't get the breaks, and there's no reason to believe I will in the future.
	11. All I can see ahead of me is unpleasantness rather than pleasantness.

12. I don't expect to get what I really want.
14. Things just won't work out the way I want them to.
16. I never get what I want so it's foolish to want anything.
17. It is very unlikely that I will get any real satisfaction in the future.
18. The future seems vague and uncertain to me.
20. There's no use in really trying to get something I want because I probably won't get it.

False 1. I look forward to the future with hope and enthusiasm.
3. When things are going badly, I am helped by knowing they can't stay that way forever.
5. I have enough time to accomplish the things I most want to do.
6. In the future, I expect to succeed in what concerns me most.
8. I expect to get more of the good things in life than the average person.
10. My past experiences have prepared me well for my future.
13. When I look ahead to the future, I expect I will be happier then than I am now.
15. I have great faith in the future.
19. I can look forward to more good times than bad times.

SCHIZOPHRENIA

One out of every ten schizophrenics dies by suicide in the United States—many times the rate for the general population.[17] Schizophrenia is a condition that is characterized by disturbances of thinking, mood, and behavior, and often by distortions of the person's ability to perceive reality correctly. As noted earlier, sometimes people suffering from this disorder form delusional ideas or experience hallucinations. In this state, occasionally a person may kill himself or herself in response to voices or in order to escape imagined persecution.

In contrast to earlier findings, recent studies of suicide among schizophrenic patients found that most of those studied did not commit suicide in a psychotic, delusional state. Some of these suicides were associated with depression, which occurs frequently in people with chronic schizophrenia. However, stress and hardships in adapting to society seem to be the major trigger for suicide among schizophrenics. As noted earlier, there is a relationship between stressful life events and suicide in the general population, but the types of events which produce the most stress are different for schizophrenics. Predicting risk may be difficult, because schizophrenics are less likely to signal their intentions to others.

Recently, some adolescents were interviewed for a television news broadcast. They were intelligent, attractive young people who had one thing in common —they had all attempted suicide. Most of them commented that they found it difficult to talk to their parents. Some parents were too busy to listen, while others laughed at the idea of a young person wanting to die. One girl said that her father had dismissed her suicidal feelings as a "phase" that would pass. A very high percentage of suicidal teenagers think their families do not understand them. These feelings are common; many teenagers feel misunderstood, but certainly not all of them attempt suicide.

GROWING UP "DEAD"

Dr. Herbert Hendin has treated many college students who have made suicide attempts, and has found that for many, death has been a way of life. They have been emotionally dead all their lives, and suicide was giving reality to a state that already existed. Dr. Hendin notes

88

that death, depression, and unhappiness seem to have been with them since childhood, and have been built into their relationships with their parents.

Many families are so full of anger and anxiety that the only way to survive is for both parents and children to bury their feelings within themselves. However, an acute awareness still remains that something is missing from their lives. For example, Jean was a talented, well-educated young woman who had been depressed for a long time because of the emptiness and loneliness of her life. She was unable to enjoy anything she did and took no pleasure in her very real artistic accomplishments.

She complained of having no feelings at all; she denied ever feeling anger or love or happiness. Jean had grown up in a family where there had been no love, trust, or other good feelings; she remembered only conflict. Both parents had been very rejecting and abusive toward her, and her mother, who had been psychotic, died when Jean was nine years old. Her mother had often impressed on her the necessity of squelching her feelings as a means of survival. Jean had a long history of self-destructive behavior, often slashing herself with a razor blade. One of the reasons she gave was that only at these times was she able to feel anything; pain was better than no feelings at all. On several occasions, Jean made serious suicide attempts, usually when she felt especially worthless and wanted to punish herself for something. Often, these attempts came after an encounter during which she had not expressed appropriate anger or annoyance at another person. She commented that she had something bad inside that she needed to kill. It turned out that the bad thing in her was the internalized image of her mother, whom she thought of as a demon or spirit in her head.

Although Jean's case is a complicated and extreme example, it points up several themes that are repeated with variations in many instances of suicide. She had a background of emotional rejection by her parents and at age nine experienced the death of her mother. During her childhood, she experienced many other stressful situations within her family. She was unable to express anger or direct hostility toward others, so she turned it inward against herself, and at the same time, against her mother. Her self-esteem was very low, and she felt worthless and incompetent. She saw herself as helpless and not in control of her own life; since she could not allow herself to express her needs or feelings, she often put others in the position of telling her what to do. In this way, she perpetuated the helplessness that she had learned as a child. Because she saw no way of changing, her future looked bleak, and her outlook on life was hopeless. Jean is a sad example of a person who has grown up dead.

HOSTILE FAMILIES

Many people have wondered what kind of family environment fosters the development of suicidal children. Some experts think that there has been an increase in hidden hostility against children in many families. Dr. Herbert Hendin, as noted earlier, has commented on the negative feelings and covert ambivalence present in the families of suicidal students whom he treated.

Often, parental attitudes appear to be very ambivalent toward the suicidal adolescent. About half of the parents in one study were found to have conveyed to their children the feeling that they were unwanted and too much trouble. Some researchers have used the term "expendable child" in this connection. Sometimes the suicide attempt seemed to have been triggered directly by a hostile or rejecting comment from a parent. Unbelievable as it may seem, there have been many instances in which the family of a suicidal youngster does not take the proper precautions and "forgets" to remove guns or drugs from the house. In these cases, suicide may be the result of carrying out the family's unconscious hostile wishes.

In other families, the emotional deprivation is not hidden. Many suicidal adolescents come from homes that are characterized by disorganization, parental disharmony, cruelty, and abandonment. In many instances, a successful suicide has two ingredients—a hostile, rejecting family, and an adolescent who cannot retaliate in any way except to commit suicide.

Some suicidal adolescents grow up in families who push their children too hard to perform at school, in sports, and socially. Often, these parents are attempting to live out their own fantasies through their children. The parents try to impose their own standards and goals without listening to what their children have to say. While both children and adolescents need and want some guidance, they need to develop independence at the same time. They also need supportive parents who are not constantly demanding perfection. Some adolescents who feel that they cannot measure up to their parents' expectations may become depressed and suicidal.

PARENTAL LOSS

Much has been written about parental loss as a factor in depression and in suicide. Studies have shown that from 44 to 66 percent of adolescents who attempted or completed suicide come from broken homes. But it is extremely difficult to assess the effects of parental loss and broken homes, because there are so many other variables at work. Parental loss may be more significant if it occurs at an early age; repeated separations may be more traumatic than a single loss. In addition, the outcome depends on the ability of the remaining parent or other family members to meet the child's needs and to deal with his or her problems.

Experts note that today's young adults face more choices and have greater freedom and fewer limits than ever before. Suicide may be viewed as an attempt to escape from, or as a way of expressing anger about, such "modern ills" as frequent moves to new neighborhoods and schools, family crises such as divorce, death, or peer pressure, pressure to achieve, a failed romance, or any other of life's stresses.

Much needs to be investigated about the complex subject of causes of suicide. This discussion has only touched on some of the important points that may play a part in growing up dead. Each case is individual.

LOOKING AT ADOLESCENT SUICIDE

Adolescence has often been called the "best time of your life," but actually it is a difficult, complex, and anxious period of development. There are few clear guidelines to help young people resolve the problems they must make in their transition to adulthood.

Adolescents go through physical, intellectual, and emotional changes while developing sexually. They are getting ready to leave their families and are forming new relationships while establishing their own identity and preparing themselves for a future in a complex and changing world. Problems in any of these areas may play a role in the development of suicidal feelings.

Many adolescents do not show any recognizable signs of suicidal behavior in the three months preceding their suicide attempts. In many instances, the precipitating event seems trivial on the surface. The suicide attempt appears to be a sudden, impulsive

92

Risk Factors for Increased and Protective Factors for Decreased Youth Suicidal Risk

Increased Suicidal Risk

⟵ Risk Factors For:

Youth Suicidal Risk

⟶ Protective Factors For: ⟶

Decreased Suicidal Risk

1. Loss of Social Support
   a. Death
   b. Parental Separation/Divorce
   c. School Changes
   d. Peer Problems

2. Variability in Parental Functioning:
   a. Affective Disorders
   b. Suicidal Tendencies
   c. Alcohol Abuse

3. Violence
   a. Sexual Abuse
   b. Physical Abuse

1. Presence of Social Support
   a. Empathy
   b. Constant Availability
   c. Limit Setting
   d. Environmental Structure

2. Individual Adaptive Skills
   a. Appraisal of Stress
   b. Seek Alternative Solutions
   c. High Frustration Tolerance
   d. Self-esteem
   e. Good Impulse Control

Source: Report of the Secretary's Task Force on Youth Suicide, U.S. Department of Health and Human Services, 1989.

reaction to a stressful situation, such as a quarrel with parents or the breaking up of a romance.

A large proportion of suicidal adolescents seem to show long-standing patterns of impulsive behavior. Many drive beyond the speed limit, accept dares, and are easily aroused to anger. Most are attempters, but some succeed in killing themselves. A number are individuals who cannot deal with their problems in socially acceptable ways. They usually deny having any problems, and many deny serious motives for their suicide attempts. Many have had suicidal ideas before. Often, there are obvious elements of revenge or spite directed against their families, or manipulative behavior— "emotional blackmail" with the purpose of arousing guilt.

Anonymous surveys of high school students have shown that almost 9 percent reported having made a suicide attempt. Two-thirds said they had not told anyone before the attempt.[18]

SUICIDAL PRESCHOOLERS

Death by suicide by preschoolers is rare. But suicidal behavior in young children is distressingly common. Some very young children who were asked about "accidents" admitted that these were suicide attempts. A suicidal group of preschoolers was compared with a group of behaviorally disordered preschoolers, matched by age, sex, race, parental marriage state, and socioeconomic status. The suicidal group showed much less pain and cried less after injury. They had greater loss of interest and more morbid ideas, depression, impulsivity, hyperactivity, and running-away behavior. More of the suicidal children were unwanted and either abused or neglected by their parents.

In another study, suicidal children had early experiences of separation and loss. Death of, or separation

94

from, a parent or grandparent, death of a sibling or pet, and loss of personal possessions were noted in 80 percent of the suicidal group. Sixty-five percent witnessed violent fights between their parents and 60 percent were physically abused themselves.

Some suicidal children think that death is reversible and see suicide as a way to reunite with a parent lost through divorce or death. Some children try to punish themselves or escape from an intolerable home life. These children tend to view death as irreversible.

Young suicide attempters use violent methods such as hanging, running into traffic, drowning, stabbing, and poisoning. Although preschool suicide is rare, families and others should take notice and take action if a young child talks about wanting to die.

SUICIDE AND
ADOLESCENT AGGRESSION

Although adolescence is normally a time of increased conflict, suicidal teenagers seem to have more difficulties than others in resolving their problems. Many have had a lifelong history of problems, with more than the normal increase during adolescence. Additional stress, such as some disturbance in a meaningful personal relationship, may result in a suicide attempt.

The relationship between suicide and aggression has been discussed earlier. According to some writers, most people are born with a "reasonable amount" of innate aggression. Individuals who have been taught to handle their aggression well are able to assert themselves in healthy ways.

Some people may be born with an unusually high aggressive drive. Others may be subject to an increased amount of frustration from their families or society, which may lead to hostile aggression. During adolescence, when there is a normal increase in aggression, such individuals may experience special problems. The aggression may be turned inward or outward. Often, these people may express feelings of hostility toward themselves and others at the same time. It is not difficult to understand the close relationship between suicide and homicide, and the not uncommon newspaper accounts of homicide followed by suicide.

SOME SPECIAL PROBLEMS

Adolescents who are prone to suicide may have more than the usual problems in attempting to find their identity and in attaining independence. Many are highly ambivalent about growing up, and remain abnormally dependent, because they equate independence with the loss of parental love. Overly dependent people are more susceptible to loss, and may react with suicidal behavior in an attempt to gratify their wishes to be cared for.

School problems have been associated with suicide in adolescents as well as children. In one study, an estimated one-third of the adolescent suicide attempters were found to have dropped out of school because of behavior problems rather than academic difficulties. The school problems in these cases were the result of long-standing emotional difficulties which were also the forerunners of suicide.

SEXUAL PROBLEMS

Suicide is the leading cause of death among homosexual and bisexual youth. It is also high among transsexuals (people who believe they have a gender identity that is different from the sex they were born with). Transsexuals may have a heterosexual, homosexual, or bisexual orientation. According to Paul Gibson, a therapist and program consultant in San Francisco, these groups may compose up to 30 percent of all completed youth suicides annually.[19]

Most homosexual, or gay, youths lack accurate information about homosexuality. They often feel totally alone and they withdraw socially because they fear adverse consequences if their orientation is known. Being open can provide some sense of security within themselves, but it may produce considerable conflict with family and peers. Those who hide their true feelings lead a double life in constant fear of being found out. In both instances, depression is common.

Although there has been some progress in our society's acceptance of homosexuality, there is still a great deal of rejection and abuse of individuals who feel a primary attraction to those of the same sex. It is apparent that a substantial number of youth are homosexual, although it is difficult to measure the percentage. Estimates range from one in four to one in ten. Some experts believe that as many as 30% of completed suicides are homosexuals.[20]

Teens who have experienced incest and other forms of sexual abuse have a higher rate of suicide. In the *Journal of the Canadian Psychiatric Association,* a study was reported in which one-third of the suicidal adolescent females interviewed had been seduced by their fathers. This experience is so painful and produces such strong guilt feelings that it is not surprising that sexual conflicts are among the problems associated with suicidal behavior. Incestuous preoccupations in girls who attempt suicide are not uncommon, according to some.

In some instances, adolescent boys have strangled themselves, possibly by accident, while engaging in activities that were sexually stimulating. Many were found with ropes around their limbs as well as their necks, and some have been dressed in women's clothing. These adolescents presumably derived sexual pleasure from acting out their fantasies. It is difficult to determine how many of those boys actually wanted to commit suicide.

SUICIDE AND AIDS

The suffering of people with AIDS has been the reason for many suicides, although most of these occur when the disease has become full-blown. Although new drugs are easing some of the pain, there are people with AIDS who prefer to die by suicide before they reach the point where diseases associated with AIDS take their lives.

Many young people become infected during their teen years. Since the virus may remain dormant for at least ten years, relatively few teens are aware that they carry it and can spread it. Testing of those at risk should be accompanied by counseling to prevent suicides. Since no cure for AIDS has yet been found, the news of a positive AIDS test should be treated like news of any catastrophic or life-threatening illness.

11
Prevention: What to Do and What Not to Do

Youth suicide is a tragic waste of life. Undecided, wavering, almost always young people who commit suicide *ask* to be saved from themselves right up to the time of death. Ask, but are not heard.

Most suicides can be prevented. You can help by knowing the danger signs, knowing what are some of the things you can say to a suicidal person, and what to do and what not to do.

Suppose Jill confides in a friend that she is tired of living. The conversation might go like this:

"I feel rotten. I might as well be dead," Jill says.

One of her friends may offer the advice, "Get it together, Jill. You can hack it."

Another friend might tell her to think how lucky she is. Their friend Mary has cancer, but she is not depressed. "And Mary may not live more than a year."

"She's lucky," is the response from Jill. That makes her friends uncomfortable, but they decide to forget it. "Jill isn't the suicidal type," they tell each other.

One close friend, in whom Jill has confided her

actual suicide *plans,* wants to keep her promise not to tell on Jill because, "Jill would never forgive me if I broke my promise." She tells herself that Jill will feel better tomorrow. Of course, that could happen.

But what if, when tomorrow comes, Jill drives her car around a curve at high speed and crashes into a large tree, killing herself? The accident upsets the whole class, but the friends who suspected her death was not an accident are shocked. They know they did not listen to Jill's hints—her cry for help. The friend in whom she confided her "secret" feels two kinds of grief: the loss of someone close to her, and the guilt and sorrow of knowing she could have told the secret to someone who might have very easily persuaded Jill that there were other alternatives.

One of the first steps in prevention is a change in attitude about suicide. We can recognize the clues and not back away. Most people who are thinking of suicide reveal their thoughts directly or indirectly, giving friends or family a chance to direct them to a source of help via phone contact with a crisis-center counselor, a member of clergy, or school counselor. There are many people offering help. You can be among them if you direct someone to professional assistance.

CLUES TO SUICIDE

Preoccupation with Thoughts of Death ▪ Verbal clues can be very faint. Someone can ask about the hereafter in connection with a third person, or talk about another person's suicidal thoughts or plans. Ideas about heaven or hell are hints about thoughts of death, even when talked about "objectively."

Statements of Worthlessness ▪ Most suicidal young people feel mild depression and suffer from poor self-esteem. Usually, an event triggers loss of faith in oneself; a

100

time of danger. These can range from a bad grade on an exam, losing an after-school job, an argument with a friend of either sex, inability to pay a debt, the loss or illness of a parent, or a change in life-style.

A Settling of Affairs ▪ Concern about life insurance, wills, and other documents can indicate suicidal plans. While many adults normally are concerned about these things, those with suicidal intent may show more obvious concern as an unconscious way of asking for help.

Giving Away Prized Possessions ▪ People of all ages may be signaling their suicidal mentality when they give away, for no apparent reason, prized possessions such as cameras and jewelry, or any variety of material things. Sometimes they remark that these things will not be "needed" anymore. Some people act as if they are going on a trip. This "generosity" should set off an alarm.

Suicide Threats ▪ The false belief that "people who say they are going to kill themselves never do" has long been disproved. "I really didn't think he (she) would do it" is a remark that is often made by people who ignored suicide threats. Every suicide threat should be taken very seriously.

Depression ▪ Common symptoms of depression are crying, sleeplessness, loss of appetite, isolation, and hopelessness. The relationship of depression and suicide has been discussed earlier. When a person is more withdrawn, uncommunicative, and isolated from others than usual, he or she may be sending out a warning signal. Question that person if necessary.

101

Possession of Suicidal Plans ▪ Question a person who appears to you to be suicidal to determine if any detailed suicide plans have been made, the details of the plan, and whether or not any beginning action has been taken. Any hints of such plans call for IMMEDIATE HELP from a crisis center.

Accidental Poisoning and Self-Destructive Behavior ▪ What appears to be accidental self-poisoning, such as pills combined with alcohol, is likely to be an attempt at self-destruction, especially in the adolescent years. If you have a friend who has had several episodes of self-poisoning, take this as a strong clue to suicidal intent. The intent may be unconscious, and therefore unclear. This friend needs counseling.

A suicidal gesture by adolescents may come before the act of self-destruction as often as three times when "accidental" poisoning occurs. In drug overdoses, drugs most commonly used are aspirin, Tylenol, Dalmane and Valium in combination with each other or with alcohol. Some of these combinations cause permanent brain damage instead of death.

A Sudden Apparent Peace of Mind ▪ Knowing the above clues is not always enough, for the clues may be missed even by professionals who are trained to understand people's feelings. In one case, a woman who was being treated by a psychiatrist for severe depression appeared to be much better. The psychiatrist was pleased with the woman's apparent peace of mind. But after the patient left the doctor's office, she went home and swallowed all the sleeping pills in the bottle next to her bed. After the suicide, the psychiatrist and others who had known the woman put together some of the clues to the puzzle and wondered why they had not recognized the warning signals. They realized the woman had resolved her conflict about whether to live

102

or to die, but that she did not express this in words. The clue: her tranquility or peace of mind.

Knowing whether or not any of the above are serious warning signals can be difficult even for a professional, but it is better to err on the side of suspicion. All of the clues or signals here, and others, are actually hints to those who really listen. Use your intuition, or common sense. Sometimes friends can recognize a suicidal intention by a change in manner. Sudden passivity, a giving up, make them "just know" something is terribly wrong. And something is. Any sign that someone is considering suicide is an alarm, a call to action. Respond.

WHAT TO DO

Believe It ■ When someone talks of suicide, he or she should be taken very seriously. Accept what is said, and try to focus on the problem. If you have a good relationship with the person, you might want to be frank with your concern. Ask the person if he or she is thinking about giving up on life, or ending it all.

Listen ■ A person who is feeling suicidal is in a state of emotional crisis and needs someone who will listen. By reflecting back the person's feelings you can help that person to feel that someone has heard his or her pain. Acknowledge the person's feelings of helplessness. You can say, "I can see how you feel." By listening, you are being supportive; you are showing you care. Ask questions, talk calmly, listen carefully, and sympathize.

Get Help ■ No matter what you yourself conclude about the intensity of the crisis, you must get help. Call a suicide-prevention center, crisis-intervention clinic, mental-health clinic, physician, hospital emergency room, or religious adviser. A reliable family member can be told, one who will get more help. If you believe the person is in danger of taking action at once, do not leave him or her. Talk about the problem and lead the person to one of the above places. If you feel that the situation is immediately life-threatening, call the police.

Remove Weapons of Choice ▪ If you learn about actual, specific plans that have been made toward suicide, you can be almost sure that the risk is greater than if they are vague. Stay with the person, if possible, and get help. Remove any self-destructive weapons the person talked about.

WHAT NOT TO DO

Do Not Give Advice ▪ Other than seeking help for the person, you should not try to offer such advice as, "Everything will be all right," or, "Snap out of it." Do not be judgmental.

Do not swear secrecy.

Do not debate whether suicide is right or wrong.

Do not increase guilt.

"Think how your parents, friends, etc., would feel" will not help a person who feels anger or helplessness. Avoid such remarks as, "Be grateful for what you have. You are much better off than most people." This can make the person feel more worthless than if you had said nothing. The last thing a suicidal person needs is a lecture. If he or she could feel empathy for other people and pull out of the depression or hopeless state, suicide would not be part of the picture.

Do Not Delay Dealing with the Situation ▪ Do not leave the person alone if you think the risk is immediate. Call a

104

suicide-prevention center. If you are not near a telephone, invent an excuse that will make the person go with you to a place where there is a phone.

Never Tell a Person that He or She Is Just Fooling ▪ Not being believed would increase despair and might serve as a challenge that could start self-destructive actions. Sometimes it is possible to deter a suicidal person by removing the weapons of choice. One might think that removing knives or guns would only change the mode of suicide, but it has been shown that many people plan to do away with themselves by a certain method and do not resort to others if that method is unavailable.

A suicide is often a matter that involves two people. Those who work at suicide-prevention centers have found that there are cases where a "significant other" is helping the suicidal person to carry out his or her wishes. This may be unconscious, or it may be blatant. In at least one case, the "significant other" has been known to have hidden a gun under the mattress of the suicidal person. Therapists are able to discover and deal with the interplay between the suicidal person and the other person involved, but this takes training. But removing obvious things that might be used in suicide plans is something that any caring person can do on finding that someone in the family has given clues to their suicide.

SUICIDE PREVENTION
IN THE CLASSROOM

A growing number of communities are accepting the idea of teaching suicide prevention in the schools as part of their health education programs. Individuals who are concerned about the possible increase in youth suicide or simply want to save even one life, can suggest such programs to their counselors, health education teachers, and principals. They can ask their parents to bring up the subject at Parent-Teacher-Association or other organization meetings.

Schools where one (or more) students have committed suicide can galvanize the attention given to the tragedy and start a teaching program. After four young people took their lives within an eighteen-month period, the Cherry Creek school district in Denver, Colorado, began a program of class discussions with students, and held parent workshops and volunteer training seminars for teachers, counselors, and nurses who work in the seven secondary schools of that district.

Students, in their seventh- and eighth-grade suicide-prevention discussions, learn the danger of keeping threats as secrets and are encouraged to tell a counselor of threats they hear. They learn to openly discuss their feelings about depression and suicide. These students know not to panic if they feel depressed or overwhelmed and how to use community resources to help themselves and others. They learn alternatives to suicide. There are ways of dealing with a painful life. All these skills strengthen them. Having those insights, and better ways to cope with life's stresses, brings these students closer together.

A parent who attended a workshop learned the way to cope with her child's statements about suicide and how to help. She asked questions about her twelve-year-old, a boy who had threatened suicide. It turned out he even had a plan to hang himself in the garage. Immediate action led to hospitalization where medication and counseling lessened his depression in a period of three weeks. A life was saved.

Teachers learn to spot suicidal themes in writing assignments and artwork and to take action to help troubled young people. Other school systems are

106

working with similar programs. All such programs broaden the students' vision of life and increase the values we call "human"—hope, imagination, and care for others.

SUICIDE-PREVENTION CENTERS

What happens at a suicide-prevention center when a person calls for help depends partly on the individual case. But in each case, the person who answers the phone concentrates on getting the caller over the crisis. As with all hotlines, there is the policy of anonymity unless the caller wishes to be identified. In the case of a suicidal crisis, the worker tries to get information about the location of the person if that person seems on the verge of taking action. Then, help can be sent. But if this information is held back, the suicide-prevention worker can ask questions and talk with the caller only in such a way that he or she calms the individual by providing emotional support, and helps the person past the immediate state of tunnel vision. Alternatives to suicide are then possible.

No one knows how many lives are saved by any suicide-prevention center. Many people who call may not be very serious about taking their lives. But in the great majority of cases, they want and need help, and this is what is available.

The number of calls to suicide-prevention centers continues to mount each year, and the number of centers is growing. Some areas are developing programs that reach out far from the counseling center. When a person who is feeling suicidal calls a prevention center, the volunteer answering the phone consults a professional who is on call to determine whether or not the situation is serious enough to bring in the crisis worker in the area. If it is, the volunteer calls the team member in the area and provides that worker with the necessary information. In some cases, face-to-face intervention is attempted by the team member and another volunteer who assists with such crises. The professional on call is kept abreast of the situation by following the communication between the volunteer in the community and crisis centers.

As with other volunteers, the community crisis workers are carefully screened, and they are trained in suicide intervention and in ways to help a person after the crisis is over. They are supervised on a regular basis just as telephone crisis counselors are, but community workers are also trained in face-to-face intervention. This technique has proved very helpful in areas where geography makes it impossible for professionals to get to places where people are attempting to take their own lives.

THE AMERICAN ASSOCIATION OF SUICIDOLOGY

In order to further the goal of suicide prevention, the American Association of Suicidology was founded in the United States in 1968 by Professor Edwin Shneidman. He was chief of the Center for Studies of Suicide Prevention at the National Institute of Mental Health at that time. Today, this association has several hundred Suicide and Crisis Intervention Centers in its membership along with individuals who are interested in similar goals. A list of these centers appears at the back of this book.

One of the important functions of the American Association of Suicidology is the development of programs and activities that can alleviate the anguish and cost of suicide. The association enlists the support of people in many professions and coordinates the efforts of individual communities in the area of suicide prevention. In addition to sponsoring conferences and publications for the public and researchers, it sponsors awareness programs. Throughout the year, media announcements help to acquaint people with the suicide-prevention and crisis-intervention services available to them in their local communities. Another major goal of the association is to educate people to better recognize and respond to suicidal behavior.

RESEARCH MAY LEAD TO FURTHER PREVENTION

Identifying risk factors has been, and always will be, difficult, since each case is different. But research is shedding light on factors that have not been considered important in the past. For example, new reports indicate that frequent panic attacks are linked to a strong and largely unappreciated risk of attempting suicide.

A panic attack is much more severe than the feelings that are often described as panic. About 3 to 4 percent of the people in the United States experience a panic attack at some time in their life.[21] About 1.5 percent of the population suffer from repeated panic attacks. Panic attacks are episodes of sudden, unpredictable, intense fear that are accompanied by symptoms such as faintness, chest pain, heart palpitations, and the sense that one is about to go crazy or die. Sufferers often seek help at hospital emergency rooms and doctors' offices. Recognizing that these recurrent attacks are known to increase a person's risk of suicide can help to prevent suicide by enabling doctors to recognize and treat the symptoms of this disorder.

The development of new stress management techniques is an important result of research in suicide prevention. Stress education is being included in some classrooms in the form of role playing that encourages students to act out typical stressful situations. Another approach is teaching students to say things in a positive manner instead of a negative one. Stress diaries are used to help students get in touch with their feelings. In these diaries, they write down how they feel and draw pictures about how stress looks to them and how it affects their bodies.

Learning relaxation techniques is another approach to suicide prevention. Dr. Antoinette Saunders, who runs a stress clinic for children, suggests a technique that is short and easy. Children are taught to identify the times when they are frightened and to remember that everyone feels that way sometimes. They are asked to "smile inside" and breathe slowly. Then they should imagine that they have air holes in the bottoms of their feet and that cool air is coming up their legs, through their bodies, to their heads. They are to hold this imaginary air for a second and then let all the stressful air out as more cool air comes in to replace it. This is just one of many relaxation techniques that teachers are suggesting for students in an effort to help them grow up with feelings of confidence.

Building self-esteem is still another technique being researched in connection with suicide prevention. One of the most popular activities used in building self-esteem is called "Car Wash." In this activity, students stand in two lines while one of them is sent through the Car Wash. Everyone touches him or her, expressing praise, encouragement, and affection. This and many other techniques to help children feel better about themselves when they are young may help to prevent suicide attempts in later years.

Admitting that the teen suicide crisis defies easy answers, Camp Fire, Inc., and the National Mental Health Association have joined forces in a nationwide youth suicide awareness and prevention program. A goal is the inclusion of suicide prevention education as a permanent part of school programs. One of the facts included in their September 1989 newsletter, *Teens in Action*, is the use of firearms by as many as 3,400 youths annually to commit suicide.

In studies of how people kill themselves, it is reported that about half of the young people who kill themselves each year do so with guns that are kept at home. What can be done to persuade parents that if they must keep a gun at home they should keep it hidden and unloaded, with bullets in a separate hiding place? Many experts believe that the urge to commit suicide lasts only about fifteen minutes. Although people who are determined to take their own lives will usually figure out a way to do so, how many lives might be saved if suicide were made more difficult? This is just one area for further research.

The enigma of suicide remains unsolved, but further research—along with increased awareness of the problem, greater attempts to prevent risk factors, and education about what to say and what not to say to a suicidal person—is a step toward reaching solutions.

APPENDIX:
SUICIDE PREVENTION AND CRISIS INTERVENTION CENTERS IN THE UNITED STATES AND CANADA

ALABAMA

AUBURN

Crisis Center of E. Alabama
P.O. Box 1949
Auburn, AL 36831-1949
Crisis Phone 1: (205) 821-8600
Business Phone: (205) 821-8600

BIRMINGHAM

*Crisis Center, Inc.
3600 8th Ave., S., Ste. 501
Birmingham, AL 35222
Crisis Phone 1: (205) 323-7777
Business Phone: (205) 323-7782

DECATUR

Crisis Call Center
No. Central Alabama MH
Center
P.O. Box 637
Decatur, AL 35601
Crisis Phone 1: (205) 355-6091
Business Phone: (205) 355-6091

HUNTSVILLE

Huntsville Helpline
P.O. Box 92
Huntsville, AL 35804
Crisis Phone 1: (205) 539-1000
Business Phone: (205) 534-1779

112

MOBILE

*Contact Mobile
P.O. Box 66608
Mobile, AL 36660-1608
Crisis Phone 1: (205) 431-5111
Tdd: (205) 431-5200
Business Phone: (205) 431-4189

MOBILE

Mobile Mental Health Center
Crisis Intervention Service
2400 Gordon Smith Drive
Mobile, AL 36617
Crisis Phone 1: (205) 473-4423
Business Phone: (205) 473-4423

MONTGOMERY

Help A Crisis
101 Colliseum Blvd
Montgomery, AL 36109
Crisis Phone 1: (205) 279-7837
Business Phone: (205) 279-7830

TUSCALOOSA

*Crisis Line
P.O. Box 2190
Tuscaloosa, AL 35401
Crisis Phone 1: (205) 345-1600
Business Phone: (205) 345-1600

ALASKA

ANCHORAGE

*#C.R.I.S.I.S. Inc.
2611 Fairbanks St, Ste A
Anchorage, AK 99503-2823

Crisis Phone 1: (907) 276-1600
Business Phone: (907) 272-2496

FAIRBANKS

*#Fairbanks Crisis Line
520 5th Avenue, Box 221
Fairbanks, AK 99701
Crisis Phone 1: (907) 452-4357
Business Phone: (907) 451-8600

ARIZONA

PHOENIX

Phoenix Crisis Intervention
Program
1250 S. 7th Avenue
Phoenix, AZ 85007
Crisis Phone 1: (602) 258-8011
Business Phone: (602) 258-8011

TUCSON

Help On Call Crisis Line
Info & Referral Service
P.O. Box 43696
Tucson, AZ 85733
Crisis Phone 1: (602) 323-9373
Business Phone: (602) 881-8045

ARKANSAS

HOT SPRINGS

Community Counseling
Services
700 South Avenue P.O.
Box 6399
Hot Springs, AR 71902

113

Crisis Phone 1: (501) 624-
7111
Business Phone: (501) 624-
7111

Crisis Center of Arkansas, Inc.
1616 W. 14th St.
Little Rock, AR 72202
Crisis Phone 1: (501) 375-
5151
Business Phone: (501) 664-
8834

Contact Pine Bluff
P.O. Box 8734
Pine Bluff, AR 71601
Crisis Phone 1: (501) 536-
4226
Business Phone: (501) 536-
4228

CALIFORNIA

*Hotline Help Center
P.O. Box 999
Anaheim, CA 92805
Crisis Phone 1: (714) 778-
1000
Business Phone: (714) 778-
1000

*#Suicide Prev/Crisis Interv of
Alameda County
P.O. Box 9102
Berkeley, CA 94709
Crisis Phone 1: (415) 849-
2212
Crisis Phone 2: (415) 889-
1333
Crisis Phone 3: (415) 794-
5211

Crisis Phone 4: (415) 449-
5566
Business Phone: (415) 848-
1515

*Suicide Prevention of Yolo
County
P.O. Box 622
Davis, CA 95617
Davis: (916) 756-5000
Woodland: (916) 666-7778
West Sacramento: (916) 372-
6565
Business Phone: (916) 756-
7542

Crisis Line-C.A.A.R.E. Project
461 N. Franklin St.
P.O. Box 764
Fort Bragg, CA 95437
Crisis Phone 1: (707) 964-
4357
Business Phone: (707) 964-
4055
Hrs Available: 24

*Help in Emotional Trouble
P.O. Box 4282
Fresno, CA 93744
Crisis Phone 1: (209) 485-
1432
Business Phone: (209) 486-
4703

*#Suicide Prevention Center
Div. Family Service of L.A.
1041 S. Menlo
Los Angeles, CA 90006
Crisis Phone 1: (213) 381-
5111
Business Phone: (213) 386-
5111

*Teen Line
Thalians Mental Health
Center
8730 Alden Drive C301
Los Angeles, CA 90048
Statewide Toll Free: (800)
852-8336
Crisis Phone 2: (213) 855-3575
Business Phone: (213) 855-3401

NAPA

*No. Bay Suicide Prevention,
Inc.
P.O. Box 2444
Napa, CA 94558
Fairfield: (707) 422-2555
Napa: (707) 255-2555
Vallejo: (707) 643-2555
Survivor's Group: (707) 544-2510
Survivor's Group: (707) 257-3470
Business Phone: (707) 257-3470

PACIFIC GROVE

*Suicide Prevention and Crisis
Center
P.O. Box 52078
Pacific Grove, CA 93950-7078
Monterey Area: (408) 649-8008
Salinas Area: (408) 424-1485
San Benito County: (408) 636-8787
Business Phone: (408) 375-6966

PASADENA

Contact Pasadena
73 N. Hill Ave.
Pasadena, CA 91106
Crisis Phone 1: (818) 449-4500

Business Phone: (818) 449-4502

REDDING

*Help, Inc.
P.O. Box 2498
Redding, CA 96099
Crisis Phone 1: (916) 225-5252
Business Phone: (916) 225-5255

SACRAMENTO

*Suicide Prevention Service of
Sacramento
P.O. Box 449
Sacramento, CA 95812-0448
Crisis Phone 1: (916) 441-1135
Business Phone: (916) 441-1135

SAN ANSELMO

*Marin Suicide Prev Center
P.O. Box 2749
San Anselmo, CA 94960
Crisis Phone 1: (415) 454-4524
Crisis Phone 2: (415) 454-4544
Business Phone: (415) 454-4566

SAN BERNARDINO

*Suicide & Crisis Intervention
Service
1669 N. E St.
San Bernardino, CA 92405
Crisis Phone 1: (714) 886-4889
Business Phone: (714) 886-6737

115

SAN DIEGO

Crisis Line
Family Crisis Intervention
 Center
5255 Mt. Etna Drive
San Diego, CA 92117
Crisis Phone 1: (619) 268-
 7777
TTY: (619) 268-7778
Business Phone: (619) 278-
 1211

SAN DIEGO

*#The Crisis Team
P.O. Box 85524
San Diego, CA 92138-5524
Crisis Phone 1: (619) 236-
 3339
San Diego Co. Only: (800)
 479-3339
Business Phone: (619) 692-
 8040

SAN FRANCISCO

*#San Francisco Suicide
 Prevention
3940 Geary Blvd.
San Francisco, CA 94118
Crisis Phone 1: (415) 221-
 1423
Crisis Phone 2: (415) 221-
 1424
Crisis Phone 3: (415) 221-
 1428
Drug Line: (415) 752-3400
Elderly: (415) 752-3778
Business Phone: (415) 752-
 4866

SAN JOSE

*#Santa Clara Suicide & Crisis
 Service
2220 Moorpark Ave.
San Jose, CA 95128

Crisis Phone 1: (408) 279-
 3312
Crisis Phone 2: (408) 683-
 2482
Business Phone: (408) 299-
 6250

SAN LUIS OBISPO

Hotline of San Luis Obispo
 Co
P.O. Box 654
San Luis Obispo, CA 93406
Crisis Phone 1: (805) 544-
 6163
Business Phone: (805) 544-
 6016

SANTA BARBARA

Call-Line
P.O. Box 14567
Santa Barbara, CA 93107
Crisis Phone 1: (805) 569-
 2255
Business Phone: (805) 682-
 2727

SANTA BARBARA

Santa Barbara Crisis
 Intervention
Psychiatric Emergency Team
4444 Calle Real
Santa Barbara, CA 93110
Daytime Hrs: (805) 964-6713
Business Phone: (805) 964-
 6713

SANTA MONICA

New Start
2400 Colorado Ave.
Santa Monica, CA 90404
Crisis Phone 1: (213) 828-
 5561
Business Phone: (213) 828-
 5561

116

Crisis Evaluation Unit
Ventura County Mental Health
Dept.
300 Hillmont Ave.
Ventura, CA 93003
Crisis Phone 1: (805) 652-
6727
Business Phone: (805) 652-
6727

COLORADO

Emergency Psych Services
1333 Iris Ave.
Boulder, CO 80302
Crisis Phone 1: (303) 447-
1665
Business Phone: (303) 443-
8500

Crisis Emergency Services
Pikes Peak Mental Health
Center
875 W. Moreno
Colorado Springs, CO 80905
Crisis Phone 1: (303) 471-
8300
Business Phone: (303) 471-
8300

*Suicide & Crisis Control
2459 So. Ash
Denver, CO 80222
Crisis Phone 1: (303) 757-
0988
Crisis Phone 2: (303) 789-
3073
Business Phone: (303) 756-
8485

Ft. Morgan Helpline
330 Meaker Street
Ft. Morgan, CO 80701
Crisis Phone 1: (303) 867-
3411
Crisis Phone 2: (303) 867-
2451
Business Phone: (303) 867-
3411

Crisis Line-A Serv of Indiv. &
Family Counseling
P.O. Box 644
Grand Junction, CO 81502
Crisis Phone 1: (303) 242-
4357
Business Phone: (303) 243-
4414

*#Pueblo Suicide Prevention
Center, Inc.
801 N. Santa Fe Ave.
Pueblo, CO 81003
Crisis Phone 1: (719) 544-
1133
Business Phone: (719) 545-
2477

CONNECTICUT

*Hotline, Inc.
189 Mason St.
Greenwich, CT 06830
Greenwich Area: (203) 661-
4357
Stamford Area: (203) 353-
4357
Business Phone: (203) 661-
4378

Info Line
900 Asylum Ave.
Hartford, CT 06105
Crisis Phone 1: (203) 522-
4636
Business Phone: (203) 522-
4636

NORWALK

*Info Line of Southwestern
Connecticut
7 Academy St.
Norwalk, CT 06850
Bridgeport: (203) 333-7555
Norwalk: (203) 853-2525
Stamford: (203) 324-1010
Business Phone: (203) 853-
9109

DELAWARE

GEORGETOWN

Georgetown Helpline Sussex
Mental Health Center
Sussex County
Georgetown, DE 19947
Crisis Phone 1: (302) 856-
6626
Business Phone: (302) 856-
2151

WILMINGTON

*Contact-Delaware, Inc.
P.O. Box 2939
Wilmington, DE 19805
Crisis Phone 1: (302) 575-
1112
TTY: (302) 656-6660
Business Phone: (302) 656-
6222

DISTRICT OF COLUMBIA

WASHINGTON

D.C. Hotline
P.O. Box 57194
Washington, DC 20037
Crisis Phone 1: (202) 223-
2255
Business Phone: (202) 223-
0020

*Fact Hotline
Family Stress Services of DC/
NCPCA
2001 O St., NW, Suite G-100
Washington, DC 20036
Crisis Phone 1: (202) 628-
3228
Business Phone: (202) 965-
1900

FLORIDA

BRADENTON

Manatee Glens Corporation
Crisis Line
P.O. Box 9478
Bradenton, FL 34206
Crisis Phone 1: (813) 748-
8585
Business Phone: (813) 747-
8648

FORT LAUDERDALE

*First Call For Help/Broward
Co
1300 So Andrews Ave
P.O. Box 22877
Ford Lauderdale, FL 33335
Crisis Phone 1: (305) 467-
6333
Teen Hotline: (305) 467-8336
Business Phone: (305) 524-
8371

Lee MHC, Inc
Crisis Stabilization Unit
P.O. Box 86137
Ft. Myers, FL 33906
Hotline: (813) 275-4242
Business Phone: (813) 275-3222

Crisis Line/Ft. Walton Beach
105 Lewis St.
Ft. Walton Beach, FL 32548
Crisis Phone 1: (904) 244-9191
Crestview, Toll Free: (904) 682-0101
Business Phone: (904) 244-0151

*#Alachua County Crisis Center
730 N. Waldo Rd.,Suite #100
Gainesville, FL 32601
Crisis Phone 1: (904) 376-4444
Crisis Phone 2: (904) 376-4445
Business Phone: (904) 372-3659

*Suicide Prevention Center
2218 Park St.
Jacksonville, FL 32204
Crisis Phone 1: (904) 387-5641
Crisis Phone 2: (904) 387-5642
Business Phone: (904) 387-5643

*Helpline, Inc.
P.O. Box 2186

Key West, FL 33045-2186
Crisis Phone 1: (305) 296-4357
Crisis Phone 2: (305) 294-5463
Middle Keys: (305) 289-1700
Upper Keys: (305) 852-1700
Business Phone: (305) 296-0129

*#Switchboard of Miami, Inc.
75 S.W. 8th St.
Miami, FL 33130
Crisis Phone 1: (305) 358-4357
Business Phone: (305) 358-1640
Hrs Available: 24

Hot Line
2900 14th St. N. #40
Naples, FL 33940
Crisis Phone 1: (813) 262-7227
Business Phone: (813) 649-1404
Hrs Available: 24

*Mental Health Services of
Orange
2520 North Orange Ave.
Orlando, FL 32804
Crisis Phone 1: (305) 896-9306
Business Phone: (305) 896-9306

We Care, Inc.
112 Pasadena Place
Orlando, FL 32803
Crisis Phone 1: (407) 628-1227

119

Teen/Kid: (407) 644-4202
Business Phone: (407) 425-
5262

Panama City Crisis Line
Life Management Center
525 E. 15th St.
Panama City, FL 32405
Crisis Phone 1: (904) 769-
9481
Business Phone: (904) 769-
9481

Teen Help Line
Lakeview Center, Inc.
1221 W. Lakeview St.
Pensacola, FL 32501
Crisis Phone 1: (904) 433-
8336
Business Phone: (904) 432-
1222

*Telephone Counsel. &
Referral
P.O. Box 20169
Tallahassee, FL 32316
Crisis Phone 1: (904) 224-
6333
Business Phone: (904) 681-
9131

*#Hillsborough County Crisis
Center, Inc.
2214 E. Henry Ave.
Tampa, FL 33610-4497
Crisis Phone 1: (813) 238-
8821
Crisis Phone 2: (813) 238-
8823
Business Phone: (813) 238-
8411

Tampa Help Line
P.O. Box 10117
Tampa, FL 33679
Crisis Phone 1: (813) 251-
4000
Business Phone: (813) 251-
4040

*Crisis Line Information &
Referral Service
P.O. Box 15456
W. Palm Beach, FL 33416
North and Central: (407) 967-
1000
South: (407) 243-1000
West (Glades): (407) 996-1121
Business Phone: (407) 967-
3110

GEORGIA

Dekalb Emergency Service
1256 Briarcliff Rd. N.E.
Room 213B
Atlanta, GA 30306
Crisis Phone 1: (404) 892-
4646
Business Phone: (404) 872-
5713

Contact Chattahoochee Valley
P.O. Box 12002
Columbus, GA 31907
Crisis Phone 1: (404) 327-
3999
Business Phone: (404) 327-
0199

Crisis Line of Macon & Bibb
Co.
Mercer University
P.O. Box 56
Macon, GA 31207
Crisis Phone 1: (912) 745-
9292
Business Phone: (912) 745-
9292

SAVANNAH

First Call for Help
P.O. Box 9119
Savannah, GA 31412
Crisis Phone 1: (912) 232-
3383
Business Phone: (912) 234-
1636
Hrs Available: 24

HAWAII

HONOLULU

*Suicide and Crisis Center
200 N. Vineyard Blvd., Rm.
#603
Honolulu, HI 96817
Crisis Phone 1: (808) 521-
4555
Business Phone: (808) 536-
7234

KAILUA-KONA

Kona Crisis Center, Inc.
P.O. Box 4363
Kailua-Kona, HI 96740
Crisis Phone 1: (808) 329-
9111
Business Phone: (808) 329-
6744

IDAHO

BOISE

Emergency Line
Region IV Services/Mental
Health Ctr
4355 Emerald
Boise, ID 83706
Crisis Phone 1: (208) 334-
6888
Business Phone: (208) 334-
6870

COEUR D' ALENE

Region I Mental Health:
Emergency Service
W. George Moody Health
Center
2195 Ironwood Court
Coeur D' Alene, ID 83814
Crisis Phone 1: (208) 667-
6406
Business Phone: (208) 667-
6406

IDAHO FALLS

Idaho Falls Emergency Service
Region VII Mental Health
150 Shoup
Idaho Falls, ID 83402
Crisis Phone 1: (208) 525-
7129
Business Phone: (208) 525-
7129

KELLOGG

Region I Mental Health
Kellogg/Wallace
140 Railroad Avenue
Kellogg, ID 83837
Crisis Phone 1: (208) 667-
6406
Business Phone: (208) 784-
1351

Twin Falls Emergency Service
Region V Mental Health
823 Harrison
Twin Falls, ID 83301
Crisis Phone 1: (208) 734-
4000
Business Phone: (208) 734-
9770

ILLINOIS

BLOOMINGTON

*Emergency Crisis Intervention
Team
Mc Clean Co Cntr for Human
Services
108 W. Market St.
Bloomington, IL 61701
Crisis Phone 1: (309) 827-
5351
Business Phone: (309) 827-
5351

CAIRO

Cairo Crisis Line
Mental Health Center
1001 Washington Avenue
Cairo, IL 62914
Crisis Phone 1: (618) 734-
2665
Business Phone: (618) 734-
2665

CHAMPAIGN

*Champaign County Mental
Health Center
Crisis Line
P.O. Box 429
Champaign, IL 61824-0429
Crisis Phone 1: (217) 398-
8080
Crisis Phone 2: (217) 359-
4141

Business Phone: (217) 398-
8080

CHICAGO

#In-Touch Hotline Counseling
Center
Univ of Illinois at Chicago
P.O. Box 4348
Chicago, IL 60680
Crisis Phone 1: (312) 996-
5535
Business Phone: (312) 996-
3490

DANVILLE

Contact Danville
504 N. Vermilion
Danville, IL 61832
Crisis Phone 1: (217) 443-
2273
Business Phone: (217) 446-
8212

EDWARDSVILLE

Edwardsville Community
Counseling Serv
1507 Troy Rd., Suite #3
Edwardsville, IL 62025
Crisis Phone 1: (618) 877-
4420
Business Phone: (618) 656-
8721

ELGIN

*Community Crisis Center
P.O. Box 1390
Elgin, IL 60121
Crisis Phone 1: (312) 697-
2380
Business Phone: (312) 697-
2381
Hrs Available: 24

ELK GROVE

Talk Line/Kids Line, Inc.
P.O. Box 1321
Elk Grove, IL 60009
Talk Line: (312) 228-6400
Kids Line: (312) 228-5437
Teen Line: (312) 228-8336
Business Phone: (312) 981-
1271
Hrs Available: 24

EVANSTON

Evanston Hospital Crisis Inter
2650 Ridge Ave.
Evanston, IL 60201
Crisis Phone 1: (312) 492-
6500
Business Phone: (312) 492-
6500
Hrs Available: 24

GALESBURG

*Spoon River Center
2323 Windish Drive
P.O. Box 1452
Galesburg, IL 61402-1452
Crisis Phone 1: (800) 322-
7143
Business Phone: (309) 344-
2323

JOLIET

*#Crisis Line of Will County
P.O. Box 2354
Joliet, IL 60434
Joliet: (815) 722-3344
Frankfort: (815) 469-6166
Bolingbrook: (312) 759-4555
Peotone: (312) 258-3333
Wilmington: (815) 476-6969
Business Phone: (815) 744-
5280

LIBERTYVILLE

Connection Telephone
Crisis Interv & Referral
P.O. Box 906
Libertyville, IL 60048
Crisis Phone 1: (312) 367-
1080
Business Phone: (312) 362-
3381
Hrs Available: 24

LINCOLN

Lincoln Crisis Clinic
Logan-Mason Mental Health
315 8th
Lincoln, IL 62656
Crisis Phone 1: (217) 732-
3600
Business Phone: (217) 732-
2161

MT. VERNON

Mt. Vernon Crisis Line
Comprehensive Services
Rt. 37 North, P.O. Box 428
Mt. Vernon, IL 62864
Crisis Phone 1: (618) 242-
1512
Business Phone: (618) 242-
1510

PEORIA

Peoria Call For Help
5407 N. University
Peoria, IL 61614
Crisis Phone 1: (309) 673-
7373
Business Phone: (309) 692-
1766

ROCKFORD

*Contact of Rockford
P.O. Box 1976
Rockford, IL 61110

123

Crisis Phone 1: (815) 964-
4044
Business Phone: (815) 964-
0400

*Crisis Services of Madison
County
21 E. Acton
Wood River, IL 62095
Crisis Phone 1: (618) 877-
4420
Crisis Phone 2: (618) 462-
2331
Business Phone: (618) 251-
4073

INDIANA

*Southwestern Indiana MHC,
Inc.
415 Mulberry St.
Evansville, IN 47713-1298
Crisis Phone 1: (812) 423-
7791
Business Phone: (812) 423-
7791

Switchboard, Inc.
227 E. Washington Blvd,
Suite 204
Ft. Wayne, IN 46802
Crisis Phone 1: (219) 456-
4561
Business Phone: (219) 424-
3551

Crisis Center-Rap Line
101 N. Montgomery
Gary, IN 46403
Rap Line: (219) 938-0900

Business Phone: (219) 938-
7070

*Mental Health Association in
Marion County
Crisis and Suicide Interv
Service
1433 N. Meridian St., Rm
#202
Indianapolis, IN 46202
Crisis Phone 1: (317) 632-
7575
Business Phone: (317) 269-
1569

IOWA

Open Line
Welch Ave. Station
P.O. Box 1138
Ames, IA 50010
Crisis Phone 1: (515) 292-
7000
Business Phone: (515) 292-
7000

*#Foundation II, Inc.
1251 Third Ave. SE
Cedar Rapids, IA 52403
Crisis Phone 1: (319) 362-
2174
In Iowa: (800) 332-4224
Business Phone: (319) 362-
1170

*Comm. Tele. Serv. Crisis Line
Service of the American Red
Cross
2116 Grand Ave.
Des Moines, IA 50312
Crisis: (515) 244-1000

124

Counseling: (515) 244-1010

AIDS Hotline Statewide: (800) 445-2437

Business Phone: (515) 244-6700

DUBUQUE

Phone A Friend Crisis Line
2013 Central, Suite 200
Dubuque, IA 52001
Crisis Phone 1: (319) 588-4016
Business Phone: (319) 557-8331

IOWA CITY

Iowa City Crisis Intervention Center
321 East First Street
Iowa City, IA 52240
Crisis Phone 1: (319) 351-0140
Business Phone: (319) 351-2726

SIOUX CITY

AID Center
206 6th St.
Sioux City, IA 51101
Crisis Phone 1: (712) 252-5000
Business Phone: (712) 252-1861

KANSAS

GARDEN CITY

Area Mental Health Center
1111 E. Spruce
Garden City, KS 67846
Crisis Phone 1: (316) 276-7689
Business Phone: (316) 275-0625

KANSAS CITY

Wyandotte Mental Health Center/County Crisis Line
36th and Eaton
Kansas City, KS 66103
Crisis Phone 1: (913) 831-1773
Business Phone: (913) 831-9500

WICHITA

*Sedgwick Co. Dept. of Mental Health
1801 E. Tenth Street
Wichita, KS 67214-3197
Crisis Phone 1: (316) 686-7465
Business Phone: (316) 268-8251

KENTUCKY

LEXINGTON

Comp. Care Center Crisis Intervention Mental Health
Bluegrass Regional Mental Health
201 Mechanic Street
Lexington, KY 40507-1096
Crisis Phone 1: (606) 233-0444
Business Phone: (606) 233-0444

LOUISVILLE

*#Crisis & Information Center
Seven Counties Services, Inc.
101 W. Muhammad Ali Blvd.
Louisville, KY 40202
Crisis Phone 1: (502) 589-4313
TDD: (502) 589-4259
KY Watts: (800) 221-0446
Business Phone: (502) 589-8630

125

LOUISIANA

BATON ROUGE

*#Baton Rouge Crisis
Intervention Center
2424 Bunker Hill Dr., #1000
Baton Rouge, LA 70808
Crisis Phone 1: (504) 924-
3900
Business Phone: (504) 928-
6482

NEW ORLEANS

*#Volunteer & Information
Agency
4747 Earhart Blvd., Suite 111
New Orleans, LA 70125
Crisis Phone 1: (504) 523-
2673
Business Phone: (504) 488-
4636

MAINE

BANGOR

Dial Help
43 Illinois Ave.
Bangor, ME 04401
Crisis Phone 1: (207) 947-
6143
Toll Free Number: (800) 431-
7810
Business Phone: (207) 947-
6143

PORTLAND

*Ingraham Volunteers, Inc.
74 Elm Street
Portland, ME 04101
Crisis Phone 1: (207) 774-
4357
TTY/TDD: (207) 773-7321
Business Phone: (207) 874-
1055

MARYLAND

BALTIMORE

Baltimore Crisis Line
Sinai Hospital
Belvedere and Greenspring
Ave.
Baltimore, MD 21215
Weekdays: (301) 328-5457
Evenings and Weekends: (301)
328-5000
Business Phone: (301) 328-
5457

Dept. of Emergency Services
Walter P. Carter Mental
Health Center
630 W. Fayette St.
Baltimore, MD 21201
Crisis Phone 1: (301) 528-
2200
Business Phone: (301) 528-
2200
Hrs Available: 24

*First Step Youth Services
Center
8303 Liberty Road
Baltimore, MD 21207
Crisis Phone 1: (301) 521-
3800
Business Phone: (301) 521-
4141

MASSACHUSETTS

BOSTON

*#The Samaritans
500 Commonwealth Ave.
Boston, MA 02215
Crisis Phone 1: (617) 247-
0220
Samariteen Line: (617) 247-
8050
Business Phone: (617) 536-
2460

126

*Samaritans of Fall River
New Bedford
386 Stanley St.
Fall River, MA 02720
Crisis Phone 1: (617) 636-
6111
Business Phone: (617) 636-
6111

*Samaritans of South
Middlesex
73 Union Ave.
Framingham, MA 01701
Crisis Phone 1: (508) 875-
4500
Crisis Phone 2: (508) 478-
7877
Business Phone: (508) 875-
4500

*Samaritans of Merrimack
Valley
55 Jackson St.
Lawrence, MA 01840
Crisis Phone 1: (508) 688-
6607
Crisis Phone 2: (508) 452-
6733
Crisis Phone 3: (508) 372-
7200
Crisis Phone 4: (508) 462-
6100
Business Phone: (508) 688-
0030

*#New Bedford Crisis Center
378 County Street
New Bedford, MA 02740
Crisis Phone 1: (617) 996-
3154
Business Phone: (617) 996-
3154

Northampton Emergency
Services
17 New South St.
Northampton, MA 01060
Crisis Phone 1: (413) 586-
5555
Business Phone: (413) 586-
5555

Pulse Hotline
P.O. Box 273
Norwood, MA 02062
Crisis Phone 1: (617) 762-
5144
Business Phone: (617) 762-
5145

*So. Norfolk Screening &
Emergency
190 Lenox St.
Norwood, MA 02062
Crisis Phone 1: (607) 769-
6060
Business Phone: (617) 769-
8670

*Crisis Center, Inc.
P.O. Box 652
Worcester, MA 01602
Crisis Phone 1: (617) 791-
6562
Business Phone: (617) 791-
7205

MICHIGAN

Washtenaw County
Community Mental Health
Center

127

110 N. Fourth, Suite 103
Ann Arbor, MI 48104
Crisis Phone 1: (313) 996-4747
Business Phone: (313) 994-2285

DETROIT

Contact Life Line
7430 2nd St., Rm. #428
Detroit, MI 48202
Crisis Phone 1: (313) 894-5555
Business Phone: (313) 875-0426

*#NSO Emergency Telephone Serv.
Suicide Prevention Center
220 Bagley, Suite 626
Detroit, MI 48226
Crisis Phone 1: (313) 224-7000
Business Phone: (313) 963-7890
Hrs Available: 24

EAST LANSING

Listening Ear of E. Lansing
547 1/2 E. Grand River
East Lansing, MI 48823
Crisis Phone 1: (517) 337-1717
Business Phone: (517) 337-1717
Hrs Available: 24

FLINT

Flint Emergency Service
Genesee Co. Mental Health
420 W. 5th Ave.
Flint, MI 48503
Crisis Phone 1: (313) 257-3740
Business Phone: (313) 257-3742

KALAMAZOO

*#Gryphon Place
1104 S. Westnedge
Kalamazoo, MI 49008
Crisis Phone 1: (616) 381-4357
Business Phone: (616) 381-1510

YPSILANTI

SOS Crisis Center
114 North River St.
Ypsilanti, MI 48198
Crisis Phone 1: (313) 485-3222
Business Phone: (313) 485-8730

MINNESOTA

DULUTH

*Human Development Center
1401 E. 1st Street
Duluth, MN 55805
Crisis Phone 1: (800) 634-8775
Business Phone: (218) 728-4491

GRAND RAPIDS

First Call for Help/Itasca County
P.O. Box 113
Grand Rapids, MN 55744
Crisis Phone 1: (218) 326-8565
TDD: (218) 326-4634
Business Phone: (218) 326-8565

MINNEAPOLIS

Contact Twin Cities
83 S. 12th Street
Minneapolis, MN 55403

Crisis Phone 1: (612) 341-
2896
Business Phone: (612) 341-
2212

*#Crisis Interv. Cntr
Hennepin County Medical
Center
701 Park Ave. South
Minneapolis, MN 55415
Crisis: (612) 347-3161
Suicide: (612) 347-2222
Crisis Home Program: (612)
347-3170
Sexual Assault: (612) 347-
5838
Behav Em Outreach: (612)
347-2011
Business Phone: (612) 347-
3164

St. Paul

First Call for Help
100 South Robert St.
St. Paul, MN 55107
First Call for Help: (612) 291-
4666
TDD: (612) 291-4630
Business Phone: (612) 291-
4666

MISSISSIPPI

Hattiesburg

Hattiesburg Help Line, Inc.
P.O. Box 183
Hattiesburg, MS 39401
Crisis Phone 1: (601) 544-
4357
Business Phone: (601) 544-
4357

Jackson

Contact Jackson
P.O. Box 5192
Jackson, MS 39296-5192

Crisis Phone 1: (601) 982-
1221
Business Phone: (601) 982-
8614

Meridian

Weems Mental Health Center
P.O. Box 4376 WS
Meridian, MS 39301
Crisis Phone 1: (601) 483-
4821
Business Phone: (601) 483-
4821

MISSOURI

Joplin

Joplin Crisis Intervention, Inc.
P.O. Box 582
Joplin, MO 64801
Crisis Phone 1: (417) 781-
2255
Business Phone: (417) 781-
2255

Kansas City

K.C. Suicide Prevention Line
Western Mo. Mental Health
Center
600 E. 22nd St.
Kansas City, MO 64108
Crisis Phone 1: (816) 471-
3939
Crisis Phone 2: (816) 471-
3940
Business Phone: (816) 471-
3000

St. Joseph

Crisis Intervention/St. Joseph
P.O. Box 263
St. Joseph, MO 64502
Crisis Phone 1: (816) 232-
1655

129

Business Phone: (816) 232-
8431

ST. LOUIS

*#Life Crisis Services, Inc.
1423 S. Big Bend Blvd.
St. Louis, MO 63117
Adults: (314) 647-4357
Teens: (314) 644-5886
Business Phone: (314) 647-
3100

MONTANA

BILLINGS

Billings Helpline
Yellowstone Co. Welfare
3021 3rd Ave. N.
Billings, MT 59191
Crisis Phone 1: (406) 248-
1691
Business Phone: (406) 248-
1691

GREAT FALLS

Community Help Line, Inc.
113 6th St. N.
Great Falls, MT 59401
Crisis Phone 1: (406) 453-
4357
Business Phone: (406) 761-
6010

HELENA

Mental Health Serv/Helena
512 Logan
Helena, MT 59601
Crisis Phone 1: (406) 443-
5353
Business Phone: (406) 442-
0640

NEBRASKA

LINCOLN

Personal Crisis Service
P.O. Box 80083
Lincoln, NE 68506
Crisis Phone 1: (402) 475-
5171
Business Phone: (402) 475-
5171

NORTH PLATTE

Heartland Counseling &
Consulting Clinic
P.O. Box 1209
North Platte, NE 69103-1209
Crisis Phone 1: (308) 532-
9332
Business Phone: (308) 532-
4050

OMAHA

The Crisis Line, Inc.
P.O. Box 4581
Omaha, NE 68104
Crisis Phone 1: (402) 341-
9111
Crisis Phone 2: (402) 341-
9112
TDD: (402) 341-9166
Business Phone: (402) 341-
9112

NEVADA

LAS VEGAS

*Clark Cty. School Dist.
Crisis Intervention
2625 E. St. Louis Avenue
Las Vegas, NV 89104
Crisis Phone 1: (702) 799-
7449
Business Phone: (702) 799-
7449
Hrs Available: 7 Hrs, Mon–Fri

Suicide Prevention Center of
  Clark Co.
3067 Greenbrier St.
Las Vegas, NV 89121
Crisis Phone 1: (702) 731-
  2990
Business Phone: (702) 731-
  2990

*#Suicide Prevention & Crisis
  Call Center
P.O. Box 8016
Reno, NV 89507
Crisis Phone 1: (702) 323-
  6111
Business Phone: (702) 323-
  4533

NEW HAMPSHIRE

*#Emergency Services
  CNHCMHS, Inc.
P.O. Box 2032
Concord, NH 03302-2032
Crisis Phone 1: (603) 228-
  1551
Outside NH: (800) 852-3323
Business Phone: (603) 228-
  1551

*#Mental Health Center of
  Greater Manchester
401 Cypress St.
Manchester, NH 03103
Crisis Phone 1: (603) 668-
  4111
Business Phone: (603) 668-
  4111

*Seacoast Mental Health
  Center
1145 Sagamore Ave.
Portsmouth, NH 03801
Crisis Phone 1: (603) 431-
  6703
Business Phone: (603) 431-
  6703

*#Center for Life Management
Salem Prof. Park
44 Stiles Rd.
Salem, NH 03079
Crisis Phone 1: (603) 432-
  2253
Business Phone: (603) 893-
  3548

NEW JERSEY

Psychiatric Intervention
  Program
Atlantic City Medical Center
1925 Pacific Ave.
Atlantic City, NJ 08401
Crisis Phone 1: (609) 344-
  1118
Business Phone: (609) 344-
  1118

Together, Inc.
7 State St.
Glassboro, NJ 08028
Crisis Phone 1: (609) 881-
  4040
Crisis Phone 2: (800) 225-
  0196
Business Phone: (609) 881-
  7045

131

*St. Mary's Community Mental
   Health
St. Mary Hospital CMHC
314 Clinton St.
Hoboken, NJ 07030
Crisis Phone 1: (201) 795-
   5505
Business Phone: (201) 792-
   8200

MONTCLAIR

North Essex Help Line
Mental Health Resource
   Center
60 S. Fullerton Ave.
Montclair, NJ 07042
Crisis Phone 1: (201) 744-
   1954
Business Phone: (201) 744-
   6522

MORRISTOWN

Helpline
Morristown Memorial Hospital
100 Madison Ave.
Morristown, NJ 07960
Crisis Phone 1: (201) 540-
   5045
Business Phone: (201) 540-
   5168

NEWARK

Newark Emergency Services
Mt. Carmel Guild Comm.
   MHC
17 Mulberry St.
Newark, NJ 07102
Crisis Phone 1: (201) 596-
   4100
Business Phone: (201) 596-
   4100

TOMS RIVER

Contact of Ocean County
P.O. Box 1121
Toms River, NJ 08754
Crisis Phone 1: (201) 240-
   6100
Crisis Phone 2: (609) 693-
   5834
Business Phone: (201) 240-
   6104

TRENTON

Contact of Mercer County, NJ
Katzenbach School for the
   Deaf
320 Sullivan Way-CN535
Trenton, NJ 08625-0535
Crisis Phone 1: (609) 896-
   2120
Crisis Phone 2: (609) 585-
   2244
TTY: (609) 587-3050
TTY: (609) 452-1919

UNION

Communication-Help Center
Kean College of NJ
Morris Avenue
Union, NJ 07083
Crisis Phone 1: (201) 527-
   2360
Crisis Phone 2: (201) 527-
   2330
Crisis Phone 3: (201) 289-
   2101
Business Phone: (201) 289-
   2100

NEW MEXICO

ALBUQUERQUE

AGORA
The Univ. of New Mexico
   Crisis Center
Student Union, P.O. Box 29

Albuquerque, NM 87131
Crisis Phone 1: (505) 277-3013
Business Phone: (505) 277-3013

Contact Lifeline
Station D Box 36184
Albuquerque, NM 87176-6184
Crisis Phone 1: (505) 266-5555
Crisis Phone 2: (505) 266-5556
Business Phone: (505) 266-5555
Hrs Available: 1PM–11PM, M–TH; 24 Hr/WKDS

NEW YORK

ALBANY

Capital Dist. Psychiatric Center
75 New Scotland Ave.
Albany, NY 12208
Crisis Phone 1: (518) 447-9650
Business Phone: (518) 447-9611

ALBANY

Samaritans of Capital Dist.
200 Central Ave.
Albany, NY 12206
Crisis Phone 1: (518) 463-2323
Business Phone: (518) 463-0861

BUFFALO

Suicide Prev. & Crisis Service, Inc.
2969 Main St.
Buffalo, NY 14214

Crisis Phone 1: (716) 834-3131
Business Phone: (716) 834-3131

GOSHEN

Orange County Help Line
Mental Health Association
255 Greenwich Ave.
Goshen, NY 10924
24HR/Helpline: (914) 343-6906
24HR/Helpline: (914) 294-9355
5–9PM/Teenline: (914) 294-9445
24HR/Helpline: (800) 832-1200
5–9PM/Teenline: (914) 565-0731

ITHACA

*#Suicide Prev. & Crisis Service of Tompkins Co.
P.O. Box 312
Ithaca, NY 14851
Crisis Phone 1: (607) 272-1616
Business Phone: (607) 272-1505

NEW PALTZ

Psychological Counseling Center
VLC 110
State University College
New Paltz, NY 12561
Crisis Phone 1: (914) 257-2920
Business Phone: (914) 257-2920

NEW YORK

Help-Line Telephone Services
3 W. 29th Street, Suite #1010
New York, NY 10001

Crisis Phone 1: (212) 532-
2400
TTY: (212) 532-0942
Business Phone: (212) 684-
4480

*The Samaritans of New York
City
P.O. Box 1259
Madison Square Station
New York, NY 10159
Crisis Phone 1: (212) 673-3000

NIAGARA FALLS

Niagara Hotline/Crisis
Intervention
775 3rd St.
Niagara Falls, NY 14302
Crisis Phone 1: (716) 285-
3515
Business Phone: (716) 285-
9636

PEEKSKILL

Peekskill Crisis Intervention
750 Washington Street
Peekskill, NY 10566
Crisis Phone 1: (914) 736-
0780
Business Phone: (914) 736-
0780

POUGHKEEPSIE

*#Dutchess County Dept. of
Mental Hygiene
Psychiatric Emergency Service
230 North Road
Poughkeepsie, NY 12601
Crisis Phone 1: (914) 485-
9700
Business Phone: (914) 485-
9700

ROCHESTER

*Life Line
Health Assn. of Rochester

1 Mount Hope Avenue
Rochester, NY 14620
Crisis Phone 1: (716) 275-
5151
TDD: (716) 275-2700
Fort Wayne County: (800)
333-0542
Business Phone: (716) 423-
9490

STONY BROOK

*Response of Suffolk Co., Inc.
P.O. Box 300
Stony Brook, NY 11790
Crisis Phone 1: (516) 751-
7500
Business Phone: (516) 751-
7620

SYRACUSE

*Suicide Prevention Service/
Crisis Counseling
Inpatient Unit 3-6
301 Prospect Ave.
Syracuse, NY 13203
Crisis Phone 1: (315) 474-
1333
Business Phone: (315) 448-
5360

UTICA

Utica Crisis Intervention
1213 Court St., Cottage 46
Utica, NY 13502
Crisis Phone 1: (315) 736-
0883
Rome: (315) 337-7299
Herkimer: (315) 866-0123
Business Phone: (315) 797-
6800

WHITE PLAINS

*Mental Health Association
Sterling Clinic MHA of West
Co.
29 Sterling Ave.

White Plains, NY 10606
Suicide Prev. Serv.: (914) 946-0121
Crisis Interv. Serv.: (914) 949-6741
Business Phone: (914) 949-6741

NORTH CAROLINA

*#Suicide & Crisis Serv/
  Alamance
P.O. Box 2573
Burlington, NC 27215
Crisis Phone 1: (919-227-6220
Business Phone: (919) 228-1720

CHAPEL HILL

Helpline C/O OPCMHC
333 Mc Masters St.
Chapel Hill, NC 27516
Crisis Phone 1: (919) 929-0479
Crisis Phone 2: (919) 732-2796
Crisis Phone 3: (919) 599-8366
Crisis Phone 4: (919) 542-4422
Crisis Phone 5: (919) 742-5612
Business Phone: (919) 929-0471

CHARLOTTE

Reachline Telephone
  Counseling
501 N. Tryon St.
P.O. Box 31603
Charlotte, NC 28231
Crisis Phone 1: (704) 333-6121

Business Phone: (704) 372-1580
Hrs Available: 24

CHARLOTTE

The Relatives, Inc.
1100 E. Boulevard
Charlotte, NC 28203
Crisis Phone 1: (704) 377-0602
Business Phone: (704) 335-0203

DURHAM

Contact Durham
803 West Chapel Hill St.
Durham, NC 27701
Crisis Phone 1: (919) 683-1595
Phone A Friend: (919) 683-3399
Business Phone: (919) 683-1568

DURHAM

Helpline of Durham
414 E. Main St.
Durham, NC 27701
Crisis Phone 1: (919) 683-8628
Business Phone: (919) 683-2392

FAYETTEVILLE

Contact of Fayetteville, Inc.
310 Green Street
Fayetteville, NC 28301
Crisis Phone 1: (919) 485-4134
Business Phone: (919) 483-8970

GOLDSBORO

Wayne Co. MHC Hotline
301 N. Herman St.

135

Goldsboro, NC 27514
Crisis Phone 1: (919) 735-4357
Business Phone: (919) 731-1133

Crisis Control Center, Inc.
P.O. Box 8663
Greensboro, NC 27419
Crisis Phone 1: (919) 852-4444
Business Phone: (919) 852-6366

Hopeline, Inc.
P.O. Box 6036
Raleigh, NC 27628
Crisis Phone 1: (919) 755-6555
Teen Hopeline: (919) 755-6777
Business Phone: (919) 755-6588

Roanoke Rapids Crisis Line
Halifax Co. Mental Health
P.O. Box 1199
Roanoke Rapids, NC 27870
Crisis Phone 1: (919) 537-2909
Business Phone: (919) 537-2909

Contact: Winston-Salem
1111 W. First St.
Winston-Salem, NC 27101
Crisis Phone 1: (919) 722-5153
Teenline, 3–7PM Daily: (919) 723-8336
Business Phone: (919) 723-4338

NORTH DAKOTA

Crisis & Emergency Services
West Central Human Services
Center
600 South 2nd St.
Bismarck, ND 58501
Crisis Phone 1: (701) 255-3090
Business Phone: (701) 255-3090

*#United Way's Hot Line
United Way of Cass Clay, Inc.
P.O. Box 1609
Fargo, ND 58107-1609
Crisis Phone 1: (701) 235-7335
Crisis Phone 2: (701) 232-4357
Business Phone: (701) 293-6462

Northeast Human Service
Center
1407 24th Ave. S.
Grand Forks, ND 58201
Crisis Phone 1: (701) 775-0525
Business Phone: (701) 746-9411

OHIO

*#CSS, Inc.
Emergency Services
513 W. Market St.
Akron, OH 44303
Crisis Phone 1: (216) 434-9144
Teleteen: (216) 434-9143

TTY/TDD: (216) 434-1706
Business Phone: (216) 434-1214

ATHENS

Careline
28 W. Stimson
Athens, OH 45701
Athens County: (614) 593-3344
Hocking County: (614) 385-8484
Vinton County: (614) 596-5211
Business Phone: (614) 593-3346

CANTON

*#Crisis Intervention Center of Stark Co.
2421 13th St., N.W.
Canton, OH 44708
Crisis Phone 1: (216) 452-6000
Business Phone: (216) 452-9812

CINCINNATI

*281-CARE: Crisis Care Center
Talbert House
3891 Reading Rd.
Cincinnati, OH 45229
Crisis Phone 1: (513) 281-2273
Business Phone: (513) 281-2866

CLEVELAND

*Citizens Mental Health Assembly
1001 Huron Road
Cleveland, OH 44115
Crisis Phone 1: (216) 781-2944
Business Phone: (216) 781-2944

COLUMBUS

*Suicide Prevention Services
1301 N. High St.
Columbus, OH 43201
Crisis Phone 1: (614) 221-5445
Teen Suicide Hotline: (614) 294-3300
Business Phone: (614) 299-6600

DAYTON

*#Suicide Prevention Center, Inc.
P.O. Box 1393
Dayton, OH 45401-1393
Crisis Phone 1: (513) 223-4777
Business Phone: (513) 223-9096

MANSFIELD

Help Line/Adapt
741 Sholl Rd.
Mansfield, OH 44907
Crisis Phone 1: (419) 522-4357
Business Phone: (419) 526-4332

OXFORD

Oxford Crisis & Referral Center
111 E. Walnut St.
Oxford, OH 45056
Crisis Phone 1: (513) 523-4146
Business Phone: (513) 523-4149

TOLEDO

*Rescue Crisis Services
3314 Collingwood Blvd.
Toledo, OH 43610

137

Crisis Phone 1: (419) 255-
5500
Business Phone: (419) 255-
9585

*#Help Hotline, Inc.
P.O. Box 46
Youngstown, OH 44501
Crisis Phone 1: (216) 747-
2696
Crisis Phone 2: (216) 424-
7767
Crisis Phone 3: (216) 426-
9355
TTY: (216) 744-0579
Business Phone: (216) 747-
5111

*Six County, Inc. Crisis Hotline
2845 Bell Street
Zanesville, OH 43701
Crisis Phone 1: (614) 452-
8403
Business Phone: (614) 454-
9766

OKLAHOMA

*Teenline
Dept. of Mental Health
Capitol Station
P.O. Box 53277
Oklahoma City, OK 73152
Local: (405) 271-8336
Statewide Toll Free: (800)
522-8336
Business Phone: (405) 271-
7474

Tulsa Helpline
P.O. Box 52847

Tulsa, OK 74152
Crisis Phone 1: (918) 583-
4357
Business Phone: (918) 585-
1144

OREGON

Mental Health Emergency
Center/CIRT
1901 Garden Ave.
Eugene, OR 97403
Crisis Phone 1: (503) 687-
4000
Business Phone: (503) 687-
4085

Helpline Referral Services
714 N.W. A Street
Grants Pass, OR 97526
Crisis Phone 1: (503) 479-
4357
Business Phone: (503) 479-
2349

Klamath Crisis Center
1014 Main Street
Klamath Falls, OR 97601
Crisis Phone 1: (503) 884-
0636
Crisis Phone 2: (503) 884-
0390
Business Phone: (503) 884-
0636

*#Metro Crisis Intervention
Service
P.O. Box 637
Portland, OR 97207
Crisis Phone 1: (503) 223-
6161

Business Phone: (503) 226-3099

SALEM

Northwest Human Services, Inc.
681 Center St. NE
Salem, OR 97303
Crisis Phone 1: (503) 581-5535
Business Phone: (503) 588-5828

PENNSYLVANIA

ALLENTOWN

Crisis Intervention Team
Lehigh County
512 Hamilton St., Suite 300
Allentown, PA 18101
Crisis Phone 1: (215) 820-3127
Business Phone: (215) 820-3127

ALTOONA

*Contact Altoona
P.O. Box 11
Altoona, PA 16603
Crisis Phone 1: (814) 946-9050
TTY Line (Deaf Line): (814) 946-1933
Business Phone: (814) 946-0531

ERIE

Info. & Referral Division
United Way of Erie County
110 W. 10th St.
Erie, PA 16501-1466
Erie Hotline: (814) 453-5656
Business Phone: (814) 456-2937

GETTYSBURG

Adams/Hanover Counseling
Services
37 West Street
Gettysburg, PA 17325
9AM–5PM: (717) 632-4900
After Hours: (717) 334-2121
Business Phone: (717) 334-9111

HARRISBURG

*Contact Harrisburg
P.O. Box 2328
Harrisburg, PA 17105
Crisis Phone 1: (717) 652-4400
Crisis Phone 2: (800) 932-4616
Business Phone: (717) 652-4987

HARRISBURG

*Dauphin County Crisis
Intervention
25 S. Front Street
Harrisburg, PA 17101
Crisis Phone 1: (717) 232-7511
Crisis Phone 2: (717) 232-7512
Crisis Phone 3: (717) 232-7513
Business Phone: (717) 255-2705

LANCASTER

Contact Lancaster
447 E. King St.
Lancaster, PA 17602
Crisis Phone 1: (717) 299-4855
Teenline: (717) 394-2000
Kids Line: (717) 291-5858
TTY: (717) 299-7184
Business Phone: (717) 291-2261

139

*Hazleton-Nanticoke Crisis
  Services
Hazleton-Nanticoke MH/MR
  Center
P.O. Box 108
Nanticoke, PA 18634
Crisis Phone 1: (717) 735-
  7590
Crisis Phone 2: (717) 455-
  6385
Business Phone: (717) 735-
  7590

Philadelphia Suicide & CI Cntr.
1 Reading Center
1101 Market 7th Floor
Philadelphia, PA 19107
Crisis Phone 1: (215) 686-
  4420
Business Phone: (215) 592-
  5565
Hrs Available: 24

*Teen Suicide Treatment &
  Prevention Program
Hahnemann University
  Hospital Mall S 403
Broad and Vine
16 So. Tower
Philadelphia, PA 19102
Crisis Phone 1: (215) 448-
  4800
Business Phone: (215) 448-
  7206

*#Contact Pittsburgh, Inc.
P.O. Box 111294
Pittsburgh, PA 15238
Crisis Phone 1: (412) 782-
  4023
Business Phone: (412) 963-
  6416

Free Information & Referral
  System
Telephone First
225 N. Washington Ave.
Scranton, PA 18503
Crisis Phone 1: (717) 961-
  1234
Business Phone: (717) 961-
  1234

Comm. Counseling Service of
  Northeast Pennsylvania
110 S. Pennsylvania Ave.
Wilkes Barre, PA 18702
Crisis Phone 1: (717) 823-
  2155
Business Phone: (717) 823-
  2155

Williamsport Helpline
815 W. 4th St.
Williamsport, PA 17701
Crisis Phone 1: (717) 323-
  8555
Crisis Phone 2: (800) 624-
  4636
Business Phone: (717) 323-
  8555

*Contact York
145 S. Duke St.
York, PA 17403
Crisis Phone 1: (717) 845-
  3656
TDD: (717) 845-9123
Teenline: (717) 845-1886
Toll Free: (800) 826-3277
Business Phone: (717) 854-
  9504

RHODE ISLAND

PROVIDENCE

*The Samaritans of Providence
2 Megee St.
Providence, RI 02906
Crisis Phone 1: (401) 272-4044
RI Only: (800) 365-4044
Business Phone: (401) 272-4044

WAKEFIELD

Sympatico
29 Columbia St.
Wakefield, RI 02879
Crisis Phone 1: (401) 783-0650
Business Phone: (401) 783-0782

SOUTH CAROLINA

COLUMBIA

*Helpline of the Midlands, Inc.
P.O. Box 6336
Columbia, SC 29260
Crisis Phone 1: (803) 771-4357
Crisis Phone 2: (803) 771-6310
Business Phone: (803) 799-6329

GREENVILLE

Help-Line/Greenville
P.O. Box 1086
Greenville, SC 29602
Crisis Phone 1: (803) 233-4357
Business Phone: (803) 242-0955

SOUTH DAKOTA

ABERDEEN

New Beginnings Center
1206 North Third
Aberdeen, SD 57401
Crisis Phone 1: (605) 229-1239
Business Phone: (605) 229-1239

SIOUX FALLS

Crisis Line
Volunteer & Information
  Center
304 S. Phillips, #310
Sioux Falls, SD 57102
Crisis Phone 1: (605) 339-4357
Business Phone: (605) 334-7022

TENNESSEE

CHATTANOOGA

Contact of Chattanooga
1202 Duncan
Chattanooga, TN 37404
Crisis Phone 1: (615) 266-8228
Crisis Phone 2: (615) 622-5193
Business Phone: (615) 629-0039

KNOXVILLE

Contact Telephone of
  Knoxville
P.O. Box 4216
Knoxville, TN 37802-4216
Crisis Phone 1: (615) 523-9124
Business Phone: (615) 523-9108

Charter Lakeside Hospital
2911 Brunswick Road
Memphis, TN 38134
Crisis Phone 1: (901) 377-4733
Business Phone: (901) 377-4700
Hrs Available: 24

*Suicide/Crisis Intervention
Service
P.O. Box 40068
Memphis, TN 38174
Crisis Phone 1: (901) 274-7477
Business Phone: (901) 276-1111

*#Crisis Intervention Center,
Inc.
P.O. Box 40752
Nashville, TN 37204-0752
Crisis Phone 1: (615) 244-7444
Business Phone: (615) 298-3359

Contact of Oak Ridge
P.O. Box 641
Oak Ridge, TN 37830
Crisis Phone 1: (615) 482-4949
Business Phone: (615) 482-5040

*#Suicide & Crisis Center
P.O. Box 3250
Amarillo, TX 79106
Crisis Phone 1: (806) 359-6699
Toll Free-in-State: (800) 692-4039
Business Phone: (806) 353-7235

*Austin-Travis Co. Mental
Health Center
Crisis Hotline
1430 Collier
Austin, TX 78704
Crisis Phone 1: (512) 440-4357
Business Phone: (512) 926-7080

*Rape & Suicide Crisis of
Southeastern Texas
P.O. Box 5011
Beaumont, TX 77706
Crisis Phone 1: (409) 835-3355
Business Phone: (409) 832-6530

*Crisis Services/Corpus Christi
4906-B Everhart
Corpus Christi, TX 78411
Crisis Phone 1: (512) 993-7410
Business Phone: (512) 993-7416

DALLAS

*#Suicide and Crisis Center
2808 Swiss Ave.
Dallas, TX 75204
Crisis Phone 1: (214) 828-1000
Business Phone: (214) 824-7020

FORT WORTH

*#Crisis Intervention
C/O Family Service, Inc.
1424 Hemphill
Fort Worth, TX 76104
Crisis Phone 1: (817) 927-5544
Business Phone: (817) 927-8884

HOUSTON

*#Crisis Intervention of
Houston, Inc.
P.O. Box 130866
Houston, TX 77219
Crisis Hotline Central: (713) 228-1505
Crisis Hotline Bay Area: (713) 333-5111
Business Phone: (713) 527-9864

LUBBOCK

Contact Lubbock
P.O. Box 6477
Lubbock, TX 79493-6477
Crisis Phone 1: (806) 765-8393
Teen Line 6–10PM: (806) 765-7272
Business Phone: (806) 765-7272

UTAH

LOGAN

Logan Helpline
121 A UMC
Utah State University
Logan, UT 84322
Crisis Phone 1: (801) 752-3964
Business Phone: (801) 750-1647

MIDVALE

Salt Lake Co. Div. of MH
6856 S. 700 East
Midvale, UT 84047
Crisis Phone 1: (801) 566-2455
Business Phone: (801) 566-2455
Hrs Available: 24

OGDEN

Ogden Emer. Services Weber
Co. Mental Health Center
2510 Washington Blvd. 5th
Floor
Ogden, UT 84401
Crisis Phone 1: (801) 626-9270
Business Phone: (801) 626-9100

PROVO

*Utah County Crisis Line
P.O. Box 1375
Provo, UT 84603
Crisis Phone 1: (801) 377-8259
Business Phone: (801) 377-8259

SALT LAKE CITY

Valley Mental Health Crisis
Intervention

143

University of Utah Med.
Center
#50 N. Medical Drive
Salt Lake City, UT 84132
Crisis Phone 1: (801) 581-
2296
Business Phone: (801) 581-
2296

VERMONT

BRATTLEBORO

Hotline for Help, Inc.
17 Elliot St.
Brattleboro, VT 05301
Crisis Phone 1: (802) 257-
7989
Business Phone: (802) 257-
7980

BURLINGTON

The Crisis Serv. of Chittenden
Med. Center Hosp. of
Vermont
Burgess Building
Burlington, VT 05401
Crisis Phone 1: (802) 656-
3587
Business Phone: (802) 656-
3587

RANDOLPH

Orange Co. Mental Health
Services
Emergency Service
P.O. Box G
Randolph, VT 05060
Crisis Phone 1: (800) 639-
6360
Business Phone: (802) 728-
4466

ST. ALBANS

St. Albans Emergency & Crisis
Serv.

Franklin Grand Isle Mental
Health Serv.
8 Ferris St.
St. Albans, VT 05478
Crisis Phone 1: (802) 524-
6554
Business Phone: (802) 524-
6554

VIRGINIA

ALEXANDRIA

Alexandria C.A.I.R. Hotline
Mental Health Assoc. in
Alexandria
3112 Mt. Vernon Avenue
Alexandria, VA 22305
Crisis Phone 1: (703) 548-
3810
Business Phone: (703) 548-
0010

ARLINGTON

*#Northern Virginia Hotline
P.O. Box 187
Arlington, VA 22210
Crisis Phone 1: (703) 527-
4077
Business Phone: (703) 522-
4460

PORTSMOUTH

*#Suicide-Crisis Center, Inc.
P.O. Box 1493
Portsmouth, VA 23705
Crisis Phone 1: (804) 399-
6393
Business Phone: (804) 393-
0502

ROANOKE

Sanctuary
Crisis Intervention
Center,
836 Campbell Ave. S.W.

Roanoke, VA 24016
Crisis Phone 1: (703) 981-2776
Business Phone: (703) 981-2791

WASHINGTON

OLYMPIA

Crisis Clinic/Thurston & Mason
P.O. Box 2463
Olympia, WA 98507
Thurston Co.: (206) 352-2211
Mason Co.: (206) 426-3311
Teen C.A.R.E. Line
(Thurston): (206) 352-3322
Business Phone: (206) 754-3888

RICHLAND

Contact Tri-Cities Area
P.O. Box 684
Richland, WA 99352
Crisis Phone 1: (509) 943-6606
Business Phone: (509) 943-9017

SEATTLE

*#Crisis Clinic of Seattle & King County
1515 Dexter Avenue North
#300
Seattle, WA 98109
Crisis Phone 1: (206) 461-3222
Business Phone: (206) 461-3210

SPOKANE

*Crisis Hotline
Spokane Community Mental Health Center
S. 107 Division

Spokane, WA 99202
Crisis Phone 1: (509) 838-4651
Crisis Phone 2: (509) 838-4428
Business Phone: (509) 838-4651

TACOMA

*Lifeline Institute for Suicide Prevention
9108 Lakewood Drive S.W.
Tacoma, WA 98499
Crisis Phone 1: (206) 584-3733
Crisis Phone 2: (206) 584-3735
Statewide Toll Free Youth: (800) 422-2552
Business Phone: (206) 584-3735

YAKIMA

Open Line
Central Washington Comprehensive Mental Health
P.O. Box 959
Yakima, WA 98907
Crisis Phone 1: (509) 575-4200
Statewide Toll Free: (800) 572-8122
Business Phone: (509) 575-4084

WEST VIRGINIA

CHARLESTON

Contact Kanawha Valley
Christ Church United Methodist
Quarrier & Morris Sts.
Charleston, WV 25301

145

Crisis Phone 1: (304) 346-0826
Business Phone: (304) 346-0828

HUNTINGTON

Contact Huntington
P.O. Box 2963
Huntington, WV 25729
Crisis Phone 1: (304) 523-3448
Business Phone: (304) 523-3447

WHEELING

Upper Ohio Valley Crisis
Hotline
P.O. Box 653
Wheeling, WV 26003
Crisis Phone 1: (304) 234-8161
Business Phone: (304) 234-1848

WISCONSIN

APPLETON

Appleton Crisis Intervention
Center
3365 West Brewster
Appleton, WI 54914
Crisis Phone 1: (414) 731-3211
Business Phone: (414) 731-3211

EAU CLAIRE

*Suicide Prevention Center
1221 Whipple St.
Eau Claire, WI 54701
Crisis Phone 1: (715) 834-6040
Business Phone: (715) 839-3274

GREEN BAY

*Crisis Intervention Center
131 S. Madison Street
Green Bay, WI 54301
Crisis Phone 1: (414) 432-8832
Business Phone: (414) 437-7071

MADISON

*Emergency Service Mental
Health Center of Dane
County
625 West Washington Avenue
Madison, WI 53703
Crisis Phone 1: (608) 251-2345
Business Phone: (608) 251-7933

MILWAUKEE

Underground Switchboard
P.O. Box 92455
Milwaukee, WI 53202
Crisis Phone 1: (414) 271-3123
TDD: (414) 271-6039
Business Phone: (414) 271-7822

WYOMING

CHEYENNE

Cheyenne Helpline
P.O. Box 404
Cheyenne, WY 82001
Crisis Phone 1: (307) 634-4469
Business Phone: (307) 632-4132

146

CANADA

Aid Service of Edmonton
203-10711 107th Avenue
Edmonton, AB T5H OW6
Crisis Phone 1: (403) 426-3242/426-4252

BRITISH COLUMBIA

Chimo Personal Distress
Intervention Service
7120 Westminster Highway
Richmond, BC V6X 1A1
Crisis Phone 1: (604) 273-8701

Crisis Intervention
and Suicide Prevention
1946 West Broadway
Vancouver, BC V6J 1Z2
Crisis Phone 1: (604) 733-4111

MANITOBA

Klinic Incorporated
545 Broadway Avenue
Winnipeg, MB R3C OW3
Crisis Phone 1: (204) 786--8686

NEW BRUNSWICK

Chimo Help Centre, Inc.
P.O. Box 1022
Fredericton, NB E3B 5C2
Crisis Phone 1: (506) 455-9464

NORTHWEST TERRITORIES

Help Information and
Distress Centre
P.O. Box 2580
Yellowknife, NT X1A 2P9
Crisis Phone 1: (403) 873-3190

NOVA SCOTIA

Help Line
c/o Dalhousie University

Coburg Road
Halifax, NS B3H 3J2
Crisis Phone 1: (902) 442-7444

ONTARIO

Canadian Mental Health
Association
Peel Branch
34 Queen Street West
Brampton, ON L6X 1A1

Military Support Centre
(F.M.O. Halifax)
2730 Gottigen Street
Halifax, NS B3K 2X0
Crisis Phone 1: (902) 427-8100

Youth Line
Huntley Youth Services
34 Huntley Street
Toronto, ON M4Y 2L1
Crisis Phone 1: (416) 967-1773

QUEBEC

St. Mary's Hospital Crisis
Clinic
3830 Lacombe Avenue
Montreal, PQ H3T1M5
Crisis Phone 1: (514) 344-3621

Tel-Aide Montreal
C.P. 205, succursale 'H'
Montreal, PQ H3G 2K7
Crisis Phone 1: (514) 935-1101

SASKATCHEWAN

Prince Albert Mobile Crisis
Unit
Co-operative Ltd.
1100-1st Avenue East
Prince Albert, SK S6V 2A7
Crisis Phone 1: (306) 764-1011

147

*Member, American Association of Suicidology
#AAS Certified

This is not an all-inclusive list of crisis centers. If you do not find a listing for your area, contact the American Association of Suicidology (2459 South Ash; Denver, Colorado 80222; 303/692-0985) for the name of the closest center. For crisis centers in Canada, contact the Ontario Association of Distress Centres (Suite 401, 99 Atlantic Avenue, Toronto, Ontario M6K 3J8; (416) 537-7373).

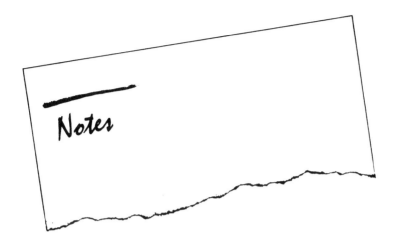

Notes

1. Nancy Merritt, *Teen Suicide*, (Phoenix, AZ: Do It Now Publications) 1988, unpaged.
2. U. S. Department of Health and Human Services, *Report of the Secretary's Task Force on Youth Suicide*, Vol. 1, (Washington, D.C.: Government Printing Office, 1989) 5.
3. *Science News*, 25 November 1990, 342.
4. *Clinical Psychiatry News*, July 1987, 11.
5. Center for National Health Statistics of the United States, 1990, unpaged.
6. *Clinical Psychiatry News*, October 1988, 6.
7. *Task Force*, Volume 3, 32.
8. *Task Force*, Volume 2, 175.
   and *Psychiatric Annals*, November 1988, 631.
9. Nancy Merritt, *Teen Suicide*, unpaged.
10. L. D. Hankoff, "Ancient Egyptian Attitudes toward Death and Suicide," *The Pharos of Alpha Omega Alpha Medical Honor Society*, vol. 38, no. 2 (April 1957) 60–64.
11. *Newsweek*, 18 June 1990, 46.
12. Ibid.

13. S. A. Applebaum, "The Problem Solving Aspect of Suicide." *J. Project. Techn.*, vol. 27 (1963), 259.
14. Avery D. Weisman, "Is Suicide a Disease?" *Life Threatening Behavior,* vol. 1, no. 4 (Winter 1971), 219–31.
15. Leland Moss, "Help Wanted: A Limited Study of Responses to One Person's Cry for Help," *Life Threatening Behavior,* vol. 1 (Spring 1971), 55–66.
16. M. Kovacs, A. T. Beck, and M. A. Weissman, "Hoplessness: An Indicator of Suicidal Risk," *Suicide,* vol. 5, no. 2, (Summer 1975), 98–103.
17. *Harvard Medical School Mental Health Newsletter,* February 1986, 3.
18. *American Journal of Psychiatry,* September 1987, 1203–6.
19. *Task Force,* vol. 3, 110.
20. Ibid.
21. *Science News,* 4 November 1989, 293.

For Further Reading

Deats, S. M., and Lenker, L. *Youth Suicide Prevention: Lessons from Literature.* New York: Plenum Publishers, 1989.

Gardner, Sandra, and Rosenberg, Gary. *Teenage Suicide.* New York: Messner, 1985.

Gordon, Sol. *When Living Hurts.* New York: UAHC Press, 1985.

Hyde, Margaret O., and Forsyth, Elizabeth. *Medical Dilemmas.* New York: Putnam, 1990.

Hyde, Margaret O., and Hyde, Lawrence E. *Meeting Death.* New York: Walker, 1989.

Leder, Jane M. *Dead Serious: A Book for Teenagers About Teenage Suicide.* New York: Macmillan, 1987.

Lukas, Christopher, and Seiden, Henry M. *Silent Grief: Living in the Wake of Suicide.* New York: Scribners, 1987.

151

Menninger, Karl A. *Man Against Himself.* San Diego, California: Harcourt, Brace, Jovanovich, 1956.

Morselli, Henry. *Suicide: An Essay on Comparative Moral Statistics.* Salem, New Hampshire: Ayer Co. Publications, Inc., reprinted 1975.

Quinnett, Paul G. *Suicide: The Forever Decision.* New York: Continuum Publishing, 1987.

Roos, Stephan. *You'll Miss Me When I'm Gone.* New York: Delacorte, 1988.

Rosenthal, Howard. *Not With My Life You Don't: Preventing Your Suicide and That of Others.* Muncie, Indiana: Accelerated Development, 1988.

Schiefer, Jay, and Rosen, Roger. *Everything You Need to Know About Suicide.* New York: Rosen Publishing Group, 1986.

Shneidman, Edwin S. (Ed.)*Suicidology: Contemporary Developments.* Grune, 1976.

Smith, Judie. *Coping with Suicide.* New York: Rosen Publishing Group, 1986.

Yochelson, Samuel, and Samenow, Stanton E. *The Criminal Personality, Vol. 3.: The Drug User.* Northvale, New Jersey: Jason Aronson, Inc., 1976.

Index

154

About the
Authors

Margaret O. Hyde is the author of more than sixty books for young people. In addition to writing and teaching, she has served as science consultant to the Lincoln School of Teachers College, Columbia University. Her previously published books include *Juvenile Justice and Injustice, The Rights of the Victim,* and, with co-author Lawrence E. Hyde, *Missing Children.*

Elizabeth Held Forsyth, a child psychiatrist, has collaborated with Margaret Hyde on several books, including *Suicide: The Hidden Epidemic.* A graduate of the Yale School of Medicine, she has served as clinical instructor in psychiatry at the University of Vermont College of Medicine and has been a psychiatric consultant for the Burlington, Vermont, public school system.

Ms. Hyde lives in Old Saybrook, Connecticut, and Ms. Forsyth is a resident of Phoenix, Arizona.